"I never realised I was trapped in a half-'whatever' until I read *The Goddess Bc* I never realised settling goes against one and success. It's not natural to be dissat The workshop elements after every ch ...allenging (it wouldn't be bootcamp otherwise!) as the book encourages you to be active – not passive – in the journey of rediscovering your power and beauty. A book I'm buying for each of my girlfriends – I wouldn't want to be the only goddess in my circles!"

~ **Sbu Mpungose**, former editor of *True Love* and *Cosmopolitan SA*

"In brief, *The Goddess Bootcamp* is all about empowered self-determination. It's definitely a self-help manual with a far more realistic outlook than most. Not only does Kagiso give a lot of herself, as she takes us through her humorous journey of self-discovery, she has left me feeling as though nothing stops me from being the best me I can ever be, despite whatever obstacles life throws in my path. I am WOWness personified!"

~ **Kay Sexwale**, radio talk show host

"Finally, a practical and truthful piece of writing. *The Goddess Bootcamp* not only celebrates our inner power and strength, but gives us detailed descriptions on how to achieve it. This motivational book stands out as one that evokes a sense of empowerment. For centuries women have always been made to feel guilty about everything from abuse to putting our needs first. I like the way the author has challenged us to put our desires to the test, to work on them, to believe in ourselves and not feel guilty. A great guide book for any parent raising a young girl."

~ **Rosie Motene**, film producer and TV star

"*The Goddess Bootcamp* gives us the opportunity to explore where we are, and where we want to go, in the various aspects of our lives and the roles we as women play in society. Don't expect to just sit back and read, but be prepared to actively do the Bootcamp. I was hooked from the first chapter."

~ **Liezel van der Westhuizen**, *Espresso* presenter

"You cannot just sit and read this book, you need to get up and DO this book. If you're not up for a challenge, put it down now. There's a feeling of quiet discomfort as you begin. It may be a feeling of knowing that there has got to be more to life than just this. You know that something has got to change, but you just don't know how to get started. Authored by a woman, and unapologetically written exclusively for women, *The Goddess Bootcamp* does not define women with reference to men; it's all about Woman Consciousness. I had many, many moments when I actually said out loud, 'Exactly!' If you were there, I would have high-fived you!"

~ **Claire Mawisa**, TV and radio personality

"Sometimes gentle and at other times not so gentle. A book filled with sessions that take you deeper into your soul's truth. Prepare to cry tears of joy and relief as you work your way to the life you deserve. Powerful sessions that peel away layers of false information to reveal the Goddess in each of us."

~ **Azania Mosaka**, *Metro FM*

The Goddess Bootcamp

The Goddess Bootcamp

Okay is a four-letter word. You are meant for more.

Kagiso Msimango

First published by MFBooks Joburg, an imprint
of Jacana Media (Pty) Ltd, in 2012
Second impression 2013; Third impression 2015
Fourth impression 2016
Fifth impression 2017
Sixth and seventh impression 2018

10 Orange Street
Sunnyside
Auckland Park 2092
South Africa
+2711 628 3200
www.jacana.co.za

ISBN 978-1-920601-04-1

Cover design by Debbie van de Merwe
Set in Sabon 11/15pt
Printed and bound by Creda Communications
Job No. 003439

See a complete list of Jacana titles at www.jacana.co.za

This book is dedicated to four goddesses:
Mary-Grace for birthing my life,
Koko for giving me the courage to live it my way,
Lebone for giving my life meaning, and
Nhlanhla for precious support and time necessary
to have a life.

"What-is-this?" he said at last.

"This is a child!" Haigha replied eagerly, coming in front of Alice to introduce her, and spreading out both his hands towards her in an Anglo-Saxon attitude. "We only found it today. It's as large as life and twice as natural!"

"I always thought they were fabulous monsters!" said the Unicorn. "Is it alive?"

"It can talk," said Haigha, solemnly.

The Unicorn looked dreamily at Alice, and said "Talk, child."

Alice could not help her lips curling up into a smile as she began: "Do you know, I always thought that Unicorns were fabulous monsters, too! I never saw one alive before!"

"Well, now that we HAVE seen each other," said the Unicorn, "if you'll believe in me, I'll believe in you. Is that a bargain?"

Excerpt from *Through the Looking Glass* by Lewis Carroll

Contents

Introduction

> The purpose of our lives is to give birth to the best that is within us.
>
> ~ Anaïs Nin

There are no coincidences.

I wrote this book because you conjured it, from a deep knowing that you are meant for a different life – one you are head over heels in love with. Hence you now hold this book I wrote for you.

I wrote this book for me too, because I am bored with hearing powerful, talented, intelligent, capable women routinely use words such as "okay", "fine", "alright", "whatever", and phrases such as "it could be worse" and "good enough", to describe, endure and justify their lives. We've ended up with pseudo lives through our willingness to settle for less, or other, than our hearts' truest desires.

I wrote this book to empower, inspire and support women to choose juicy lives of pleasure, passion and purpose, where "WOW!" moments are the rule and "OK" moments the exception.

Women are the world's biggest untapped natural resource. Alas, we are mainly ignorant of our value and power. We could be likened to a subsistence farmer who works himself to the bone, surviving on the bare necessities. All the while, the land he owns is teeming with precious natural resources and, if he knew diamonds lay beneath his rugged hands, his life would change in an instant – if he so wished.

Bruce Muzik, an international success coach from South Africa, likes telling the story of time he spent living in a township. During a personal development seminar, he uncovered a fear of black people. To conquer this fear, he accepted a challenge to move to the Cape Town township of Gugulethu for a month. He ended up living there for six months. Word got around about the *Umlungu* living in the township and people came to see him. Many asked him for money. Initially, he gave it to them, but after a while – realising that he had turned into the local ATM – he refused. Instead, being a successful entrepreneur, he offered to teach the people how to make their own money. Bruce says in those six months only one person took him up on the offer. Yes, out of hundreds of poor people who had an opportunity to empower themselves, only one took up the offer. Three hundred years of oppression had taught black South Africans that they were inferior, unworthy and incapable of being, doing and having certain things. In some cases – as with Bruce's township neighbours – this conditioning was so ingrained that people didn't even try to seize an empowering opportunity that presented itself on their doorstep, in a democratic South Africa. After only a few hundred years of institutionalised disempowerment, many black South Africans have internalised it. Now consider that femininity has been demoted, demeaned, and degraded for millennia – overtly, now only in a few countries, but in sophisticated and subtle ways, in many more. Imagine the damage of thousands of years of feminine oppression on our sense of worth and power as women! As a life coach, specialising in the personal development of women, I see how much we struggle with internalised disempowerment. What disturbs me most is that we are generally unaware of it, making its effects insidiously potent.

2

As they say at AA, awareness is the first step to recovery. You conjured this book because you are ready to recover.

My fellow sisters remind me of circus elephants – and it has nothing to do with Chicken Licken hot wings consumption. The elephant is the biggest land mammal in the world, weighing around 5 500 kilograms. It can uproot a tree without breaking a sweat, yet in the circus they are restrained with a length of rope around the ankle, secured simply around a wooden peg driven into the soil. When the elephants are still lightweight infants they tie them to very solid posts. The baby elephants fight their restraints hopelessly, to the point of exhaustion. By the time they are big enough to free themselves easily, they have long stopped trying, and their formidable mass counts for naught. The elephants settle into a life of perfecting tricks for the amusement of circus patrons. Seldom does it cross the circus elephant's mind that it does not have to be at the mercy of a 10 centimetre wooden peg nailed into the ground, or a puny ringmaster with a whip and treats.

You conjured this book to lead you away from your life of quiet desperation. There are many women who fight hard to be, do and have more. These are women who, like the baby elephants, can still feel the discomfort of their shackles. Often these are women fighting for survival, victims of various forms of abuse at the hands of those who control the resources they need for survival. They are often uneducated, unskilled and isolated, with no support structures or ideas on how to achieve emancipation and empowerment. If you are reading this, it is extremely unlikely that you are one of these women. You are more inclined to worry about the calories in your food than where your next meal is going to come from. You may fear the emotional pain of a failed relationship, but not whether leaving it means that you and your kids are going to starve. Sex is by no means your only money-making avenue. You are possibly in a worse situation: the numbing land of OKness. People experiencing extreme discomfort and acute pain fight for relief. Those who are slowly being consumed by a comfort zone, on the other hand, tend to fade out with nary a whimper. I see you, tangled up in your professionally teased hair, glued to your

3

manicured French tips, boxed in your shiny car, malnourished by your Tasha's lunches, suffocated by your winning husband, owned by your well-paying job, mesmerised by a succession of award-winning malls, trapped behind security booms, fears, insecurities, schedules and exhaustion; living a circus elephant's life. Ask yourself if you are the four-metre tall, five-ton elephant who spends her life balancing on a beach ball, because it's okay, it could be worse, it's fine, whatever…

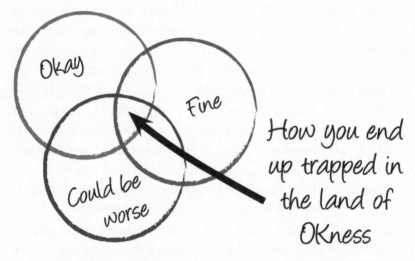

You conjured this book because you deserve a life that is worthy of you. Almost a decade ago, I was sitting in a homeopath's waiting room when a matronly Lebanese woman sized me up, declared me much too thin and offered me a banana. It was an order, really. I took the banana, even though I cannot stand them – bananas not Lebanese women. As I contemplated how to escape the banana, she demanded to know why I was so emaciated. I delivered the highlights and lowlights of the tumultuous relationship I had recently managed to claw my way out of. When I was done, she looking me sternly in the eye, while peeling the banana for me, and said, "What you need to do is get yourself better for the relationship that is worthy of you." A relationship that is worthy of me. That was such a novel concept. I had never looked at deservability from that angle. Do you ever wonder if your job, friends or partner deserves you? Is your life worthy of you? I took the banana woman's advice to heart. I sought not just a relationship, but a life that was worthy of me. I stopped wondering what I deserved and asked instead what deserves me.

You conjured this book to remind you that there is another life looking for you, one that is a perfect match for your talents, passions, values and desires. This life is calling out to you, but you can hardly hear it because of the noise from all the activity you are distracting yourself with – the distractions you have cultivated to help you forget that you have settled for less than you wanted, less than you still want. It tugs at you as you fly past in the cloud of constant busyness that you have so cleverly created so you won't have time to notice that you have settled for something other than you wanted, other than you want, still. Your life pines for you. It has sent this book to remind you that you are meant for something better, different. I wrote this book to remind you that "fine" is how you describe the weather not the life of one as formidable as you. You are not meant for this barren land of OKness. You are by birth a citizen of the land of WOWness, where it is the norm to be besotted with the life you inhabit.

You conjured this book to remind you that you are a goddess. Say it: "I am a goddess," and sense the recollections it dislodges in your soul. Dismiss the frilly and frivolous associations planted in your head of saccharine pinks, purples and teals; feather boas, diamonds and glitter; champagne bubbles, cupcakes and pretty shoes; pink vibrators and pole-dancing classes. Instead recall what you know: that a goddess is awesome, divine, blissful, respected, admired, wilful, deep, strong, purposeful, impactful, sovereign, powerful... and that you are one. This book is your golden ticket to goddess bootcamp; where you may walk in a circus elephant, desperate housewife or stressed-out executive, but if you put in the work, you will be restored to a goddess in love with her life.

I wrote this book because our messy world is crying out for a good tidying up. You may be thinking, "This is not what I signed up for, I can barely stick to a low-carb diet and she wants me to sort out the world!" Fret not, recruit, changing the world may not be easy, but it is simpler than you imagine. You change the world by changing you. You pull your tribe up by raising your own personal standards. You lead by shining. You inspire by doing *you* really well. If you choose not to settle, you make it easier for someone else to do likewise. That is all you need to do – choose better for yourself. Choose WOWness. Choose a life absolutely brimming with pleasure, passion and purpose. Choose a life worthy of a goddess.

I wrote this book to change the world, one sleeping goddess at a time. I wrote this book for us.

Kagiso M Msimango
Ambassador of Womanly WOWness

How to Make the Most of Goddess Bootcamp

Recruit, welcome to Goddess Bootcamp.

The very first thing you need to do is acquire a journal. This is crucial. You will get very little out of this book if you read it as if it's a novel. This is not a storybook; this is bootcamp. Physical, mental, emotional and spiritual exercises will be expected of you. It's not reading this, or any other, book that will magically transform your life into one worthy of a goddess. It is doing. Action. The alchemy that changes knowledge into wisdom is found in working the information.

Go get that journal. I can wait. Make it one that appeals to your aesthetic sense; you will be spending a lot of time with it, so it may as well be pretty.

Print out a really gorgeous picture of yourself and paste it on the inside front cover. Take a moment to truly think about why you are in bootcamp. What do you intend to achieve through this process? Take a moment to become very clear on your intention for reading this book. Alongside your picture, write out your intention in the present or, even better, in the past tense – as if you have already accomplished it. Write the date next to your intention. Sign it. Do whatever you need to do to make it feel like a commitment. Find a few worthy people to share your intention with. Goddess bootcamp is no place for self-help junkies who can quote Deepak Chopra, Iyanla Vanzant, Eckhart Tolle, Oprah Winfrey and Paulo Coelho but have nothing to show for it other than quotable quotes. This is not how we roll. Bootcamp is about results. The information in here is accompanied by actions designed to empower, inspire or support you in creating that life that is worthy of you. They are all very simple, but not necessarily easy. It is never easy to draw the most out of yourself; it requires going beyond the sanctioned mediocrity of our society.

Apparently Donald Trump – of the ugly hair and pretty bank balance – sees only two types of people: players and spectators. The difference is that players get paid to play the game, while spectators pay to watch the game. To get paid in bootcamp, you have to be a player. Here is how to play goddess bootcamp:

- Throughout bootcamp I ask you to write things down, a lot. I mean it. When I ask you to write something down, don't just think about it. Write it down in your journal. Writing forces you to engage and develop your thoughts. It brings them form, and gives them substance. They become more real for you.
- I ask a lot of questions. This is deliberate. Pause and answer them.
- Drop your learning barriers. There are two main barriers to learning. The first one is "I already know that", the second is "I don't agree with that". Whenever the former thought arises, ask yourself what you have done with the information; you may already know what I am talking about but have you made any use of it? As you will discover, bootcamp is all about self-examination and discovery. Be curious about yourself, your thoughts, actions and circumstances at all times. When you think "I don't agree with that", then don't, but keep an open mind. On occasion I will ask you to do pretty off-the-wall things. Remember, nothing changes unless something changes.

Whenever either of these two barriers arises, do not allow them to thwart your journey. Maintain an open mind and use them to learn more about yourself.

- Do not believe me. The information I share has had a positive impact on my life and the lives of many others, so I would like you to take it seriously, but only seriously enough to give it an honest try. I would like you to walk around in this information, as if you were trying on a pair of shoes, before you decide whether it is appropriate for you or not.

- There are actions at the end of each session, do them. They are the most important part of bootcamp. Make use of every single opportunity to actively interact with this information as opposed to merely reading it passively. There is a huge difference between knowing the path and walking the path. If there weren't, we'd all learn how to cook gourmet meals just by reading recipe books or watching *Masterchef* while lying on the couch. Apply the information and do the exercises. Even when something doesn't sound like it is important or that it's of any value, do not just dismiss it. The only way to get value from this information is through application.

- There is a lot of repetition in the book. This is deliberate. Don't skip past something because it sounds like you've read it before. Repetition increases the chance of learning. Remember having to recite the times table in that creepy sing-a-long voice in primary school? Now you know that 7 x 3 is 21.

There is a flow to how the sessions are laid out, but allow your intuition to lead you. The way of the feminine is seldom linear. Femininity is intuitive; it meanders and follows inspiration, not logic. If your inner wisdom is not keen on taking the linear route, go with it.

An alternative approach

Read through the entire book without bothering with any of the exercises or writing stuff down. It is a very easy read, so this should be quick. Then identify three sessions to which you felt the most resistance, i.e., you had a strong aversion to the information, or you struggled to get through it. Re-read each of those sessions and do the exercises religiously, for 40 days per session. I guarantee that in those 120 days your life will change in ways you would not have imagined, all positive.

Welcome to Goddess Bootcamp.

Let's go!

Seek the Goddess

Women have been taught that, for us, the earth is
flat, and that if we venture out, we will fall off the
edge.

~ Andrea Dworkin

Where should we begin our path to the
juicy land of WOWness?

Let us start at the beginning and, when we get to the end, we'll
stop.

There we find God, but before we get to Him, let me share some
trivia with you. Did you know that sprinting a mile in less than
four minutes was considered impossible, until Roger Bannister did
it on 6 May 1954? Incredibly, within three years, 16 other people
also achieved this "impossible" feat. It is amazing what you can
achieve when you have someone to look up to, a role model who
can bring out the best in you.

Role models inspire us to aim for and achieve dreams that

would otherwise have seemed beyond our reach. Whitney Houston witnessed her cousin, Dionne Warwick, release hit after hit and dreamed of being just like her. She went on to become the most awarded female artist of all time. Renowned film director Woody Allen says he watched the Marx Brothers' films hundreds of times and imagined himself being just as funny and talented. He is now an award-winning screenwriter, director, actor, comedian, author and playwright whose career has lasted for more than half a century.

Often, the influence of role models is starker when it is negative; such as when boys who have only hip hop videos and local criminals as beacons of success aspire to thuggery, or girls try to metamorphose into skinny blondes with flowing locks, thanks to a surfeit of images of airbrushed Barbie clones and not enough of women who look like them. It is well researched and documented that the Barbie image favoured by toy manufacturers, fashion houses and advertising agencies has had a significant negative impact on many women's self-image, but few have examined the even greater damage to girls and women resulting from the lack of a God in our own image. The most prevalent religions of our time portray God as male, and is God not the ultimate role model? Where do you go after God, how much higher can you aspire?

The impact of the lack of a god in our, female, image has carved a deep scar in women's self-worth and clipped our wings. This is the ultimate glass ceiling. We are in the business of creating; every day we all wake up and engage in various activities. What we are really doing is creating our lives. What do you associate creation with? For many people creating is God's domain. God is the ultimate creator, who populates the universe the way we populate our lives. When it comes to creating, God is the boss.

I grew up in a Christian household and, while I was still really young and impressionable, someone bought me *My First Book of Bible Stories*. The depiction of God in that book is still emblazoned on my psyche. God was a portly, bearded old white man, with a smiling, rosy-cheeked face. I think the same guy moonlights as Santa Claus. I was happy to pray to this God in my youth, but as my years and self-awareness increased, so did the distance between me and this "father who art in heaven". I struggled to see how an old white man, who hadn't bothered to visit earth since biblical times, would relate to or care about my problems as a young, black female earthling. The potency of a role model depends on how much of yourself you can see in them. A black, homeless, teenage prostitute shooting up heroine to get through the night is unlikely to be inspired by a middle-aged, white middle-class banker's victory over a cocaine addiction.

The first woman we meet in the old testament of the Bible, which is common to both the Christian and Jewish faiths, is Eve – and hers isn't a warm and fuzzy tale of sunflower fields, summer love and bounding golden Labrador puppies. It starts off happily enough, in the Garden of Eden, until Eve falls for the charms of a devious snake. This leads her to defy her father, God, by eating the fruit of the tree of the knowledge of good and evil – which happens to be the only thing she and hubby Adam are forbidden to do. She seduces poor Adam into breaking God's only rule. This pisses God off no end and gets them kicked out of paradise for good; dooming all their progeny – that's you and me – to lives of pain and suffering.

No wonder our world is so misogynistic, what with all the assaulting, raping, pimping, trafficking, mutilating and stoning that seems to plague women. Thanks a lot, Eve!

The damage this story has inflicted on the self-worth of women is staggering. As Laurie Sue Brockway reflects in her book, *A Goddess Is a Girl's Best Friend*,[1] "The blame, shame and underlying fear of retribution has, unfortunately, become ingrained in us even if we rarely, if ever, give it conscious thought. Whether we know it or not, women come into the world fulfilling an ancient, unconscious agreement that we are not as good as men, not as worthy and certainly not as divine. This cultural socialisation impacts us all in some way, on some level. As the daughters of Eve, we carry on her legacy." Men have an abundance of divine role models, while we have a vividly tragic cautionary tale tattooed on our collective psyche that subconsciously sends us to the naughty corner whenever we dare to want more. We learn from this story that women are fickle, unworthy, deceptive, disobedient, ungrateful, untrustworthy, evil seductresses and harbingers of doom. It is because the first woman did not stay in her lane that life is a bitch, bitch.

We've all had a conversation with a man during which he readily expressed that women are deceptive. How can men and women have healthy relationships, of any nature, with such underlying beliefs? Because men and women are products of the same history, women also carry this belief that at our very core lurks a devious Jezebel. Too often you will hear a woman proudly declare that she doesn't have female friends because women are jealous, malicious gossipmongers. Men are just as gossipy, jealous and malicious. In fact, I generally get my best scoops from men. The difference is that men keep their hands in their pockets and furrow their brows when they dish the dirt, and they never go around bragging that they do not have any male friends. You'd view a man who proudly avoids cultivating male friendships with suspicion, yet we seldom bat a Maybellined eyelash when a woman expresses such a sentiment. Why is that?

It is worthwhile, as a woman attempting to shake off Eve's shackles of guilt, to keep in mind that history is subjective. Recorders of history always edit reality based on their conscious and subconscious agendas. People tend to "see" things based on their particular frame of reference. Perception is the process by which we categorise and interpret information. Selective perception describes how we process information in a way that favours one interpretation over another; generally we interpret information in a way that is congruent with our existing values and beliefs. Psychologists say selective perception occurs automatically. The Bible is a HIStory book. Many of us tend to think that it descended, fully formed from heaven, untouched by human hands. No sister, it was compiled by mortal men, and not too long ago, either. Remember too that the Old Testament was originally written in Hebrew and the New Testament in Greek. If you've ever watched a soapie with sub-titles you will appreciate how much can get lost in translation. Yes, gorgeous daughter of Eve, my intention is to sow doubt. I usually put many people out of joint with this topic. Once I even managed to get rebuked "In the name of Lord Jesus!" I didn't even know what being rebuked meant. I do now, and I am okay with being rebuked because I like to think Jesus would approve of me advocating a cultivation of self-love. Daughter of Eve, I hope you see the purpose for which this is intended. It is important for women to seek an empowering HERstory. If we can tell a different, better story about women, it will allow us to embrace our inner power and raise our self-worth without the subconscious fear that our actions will spiral humanity down into eternal pain and suffering, again. That's a huge chip to have on your shoulder.

Patriarchal religions, in the greater scheme of things, are a recent development. There was an era when matriarchy dominated, which – although different from the current scenario – was no better. What the world needs is wholeness, not domination of one or the other. Many millennia ago, even before matriarchy, God was perceived as both male and female, Mother/Father God. Even the Old Testament occasionally forgets to keep God male. Genesis 1:26–27 reads: Then God said, Let us make mankind in **our** image, in **our** likeness, so that they may rule over the fish in the sea and the birds in the sky, over the livestock and all the wild animals, and over all the creatures that move along the ground. So God created mankind in his own image, in the image of God he created them; **male and female** he created them.

Mother Goddess is found in many ancient cultures: Greek, Roman, Tibetan, Hindu, Yoruban, Babylonian, Egyptian, Zulu and more. In his book *Indaba, My Children*, respected tribal historian Credo Mutwa retells a Zulu creation story of how the human race was created by Ninavanhu-Ma, the Great Mother. It is only in the past few millennia that God became a guy, in line with the suppression, oppression and devaluation of the feminine. I am referring to more than the oppression of women; this is the oppression of femininity in both men and women, by both genders! Take a walk through a bookstore and notice the sheer volume of

15

books teaching women how to manage, date, or think like men, which we buy. You will struggle to find 10 books teaching men to do anything like women. When a woman is likened to a boy or man it is perceived as complimentary, but most times when a man is likened to a girl or woman it is usually intended as an insult. Women insult a guy by telling him to "man up" or by referring to him as someone's bitch. Yes we do.

After centuries of racial discrimination, many black people suffered from a "white is right" mentality. Activists such as Steve Biko and Malcolm X understood that one of the elements required to correct the damages of racial oppression was for black people to recognise this thinking within themselves, and to actively and consciously cultivate black pride. Many black South Africans still suffer from internalised apartheid 18 years into our democracy. Of course, 18 years of democracy is not enough to erase the psychological effects of 300 years of colonisation, followed by 48 years of apartheid. Similarly, due to 6 000 years of feminine oppression, both men and women suffer from a "male is right/ female is wrong" mentality – bitches, witches, bimbos and hos. To free ourselves from these shackles, we need to feel them cutting into our wrists and weighing down our ankles. We can then liberate ourselves by actively and consciously cultivating feminine pride.

In order for us women to manifest lives that are worthy of us, we must acquire a healthy relationship with our personal power and self-worth, along with a healthy sense of entitlement. We too need to feel that we are legitimate heirs to the throne. I am not asking you to drop your religion, if you have one, in favour of worshipping a female god. I'd like you to acknowledge the absence of the feminine aspect of God from modern history. Recognise its impact and seek to put the feminine back into the divine, for yourself.

When I teach my daughter, Miss B, about Spirit and creation, I refer to Mother Goddess and Father God. In *Goddess: A Celebration in Art and Literature*,[2] Jalaja Bonheim observes, "Women need images that validate their femininity, their sensuousness, and their mysterious magic, and that reveal the sacred dimensions of their own gender. It's only natural that the goddess should have special significance for women, who long to know, too, that they are made in divine image." If we are all created in the image of God, then does it not follow that God has many images? I am not an old white man. The colour of my skin does not match the pallor of the God of Abraham. It is brown like that of Yoruban Goddess Oya. I cannot trace my feminine curves in the images of the form of the prevailing male God. I find them in the depictions of Venus, the Roman Goddess. When I have concerns about safety, security and survival issues, I am drawn to look to Father God for guidance and protection. When my worries are of a feminine nature, like when I am fretting about my child's health, I seek comfort from Mother Goddess.

The Goddess is hidden in plain sight. Notice her. When you drive down the highway and you are suddenly met by a burst of those pink and white flowers that grow wildly and abundantly in glorious contrast to the grey tarmac, are you not seeing the handiwork of Goddess?

Mother Goddess can still be found under different guises. Did you know that the Catholic saint St Brigit is actually co-opted from goddess worship? She is a remixed version of the Celtic triple goddess Brigid, known as the keeper of the sacred fire. The name Easter comes from the goddess Eostre, a Teutonic goddess of fertility and new beginnings. Incidentally we also have her to thank for the name of the female hormone oestrogen.

Seek the Goddess in women who own their power, women like Madonna, Oprah and Maya Angelou. Whether you are a fan of these women or not is immaterial, the fact is that their lives are self-determined; they flourish on their own terms and have a healthy sense of entitlement. There is no doubt that they feel 100 per cent comfortable and worthy of their queendoms. Madonna, who is now in her fifties, unapologetically has affairs with young men who have all their hair, rock-hard abs and butts you can bounce a coin off. How many women do you think secretly envy her for having the chutzpah to do that? The poems created by Maya Angelou can charm the hidden goddess out of the most shamed of Eve's daughters.

My favourite is "Still I Rise". Read this excerpt Evelet, and allow it to coax out your inner goddess.

Out of the huts of history's shame
I rise
Up from a past that's rooted in pain
I rise
I'm a black ocean, leaping and wide,
Welling and swelling I bear in the tide.
Leaving behind nights of terror and fear
I rise
Into a daybreak that's wondrously clear
I rise
Bringing the gifts that my ancestors gave,
I am the dream and the hope of the slave.
I rise
I rise
I rise

Plenty of women have shaken off Eve's guilt and shame. They are not all famous celebrities. For instance, one of the most powerful and grounded women I know is my grandmother. When that woman walks into a room you actually have a visceral reaction to her presence. She does not doubt her divinity, and hence allowed me an early glimpse at mine.

Seek the goddess within you, and you will find your personal power.

Becoming a Goddess: Finding the Divine Feminine

1. Seek the Goddess in Nature. Take nature walks, go hiking, go for a swim in a stream, river or ocean. Stop and smell the flowers, literally. Notice butterflies and dewdrops on spider webs early in the morning. Notice how she decorates sunsets

with pinks, oranges and purples. Take a picture of all these wonders of Gaia and paste them in your journal.

2. Seek the Goddess in history. There are many more examples of goddesses hidden in plain sight, like those of Brigid and Eostre. A fun one to go searching for is Mary Magdalene, the supposed biblical prostitute. Go on an adventure to seek out her true HERstory.

3. Seek the Goddess in modern women. The nice thing about the age we live in is that you don't have to relocate to North America to benefit from the divine presence of Marianne Williamson; you can befriend her on Facebook or follow her on Twitter. You don't need to turn back time to be inspired by the courage of Anaïs Nin; you can still read her books and connect (physically or virtually) with her other admirers. Even in your own backyard there are surely many women who have a great connection with their divinity. Befriend them. Let them inspire you.

4. In your journal, write a list of all ALL the things that you want. Check if there are any that you feel you shouldn't want – ones that feel like you want "too much", like you are asking for a bite of the apple, the one thing that God said you can't have. Acknowledge this and start pondering what needs to happen for you to give yourself permission to have these things.

5. Must Read: Michael Tellinger's *Slave Species of god.*

6. Revisit the story of Eve. In your journal:
   a. List all the beliefs and conclusions you have made about yourself, women in general, and Eve, as a result of this story. Our self-worth is determined by what we believe about ourselves. You cannot understand or change your sense of self-worth if you are not aware of your beliefs.

b. List what you love about the story, e.g., Eve had a sense of adventure, she was curious, she was persuasive enough to talk Adam into a big act of disobedience, she looked good in a fig leaf. Revision it, so you can be a proud daughter of Eve.

7. Divine Inspiration: Get acquainted with different creation myths. There are many with female goddesses as primary or equal participants in the creation of our world. On page 231 you'll find short CVs of Spider Woman, Ixchel and other goddesses who had a hand in the creation of the cosmos.

Happen to Life

The most common way people give up their power is by thinking they don't have any.

~ Alice Walker

What's happening, Evelet?

Evie, I would like to share with you a curious thing that happened to me some time back. I had recently got back into social circulation after half a decade of hibernation. I'd spent a few years being inwardly focused, immediately followed by two of consuming motherhood. I was finally out and about again, meeting a lot of people I hadn't seen in ages. Many remarked that I looked good and seemed very happy. In my twenties I was one of those girls whose life was one big drama-fest, so emerging on the other side "seeming happy" was worth commenting on. For the record, I didn't just seem happy, I was. Following this observation, people would often ask, "So, what happened?" I gave fanciful responses such as "I'm happy because I am underworked and overpaid" or

"I'm sleeping with a tantric sex master". Damn lies, but I gave them because I'd learned very quickly that they were much better received than the truth. Would you like to hear the truth about what happened to me, resulting in my aura of contentment?

Okay, here it is – drum roll – nothing, nada, zilch. Absolutely nothing happened to me. I did not win the lotto. I did not get hold of an unlimited supply of happy pills, nor bag a man hotter than George Clooney, richer than Warren Buffet, with Sting's alleged tantric sex skills, Idris Elba's broody masculinity and Ryan Gosling's... what is that thing about Ryan Gosling? Evie, if I stumble across such a man I'd have to go into another season of hibernation, for entirely different reasons. I digress. Something did happen, but it did not happen to me, I happened to it. I took responsibility for my happiness, my life and everything in it. Basically, I chose joy.

The Spanish painter Pablo Picasso, one of the most influential artists of the 20th century, once made a deliciously controversial statement about women. Women featured prominently in Picasso's life and art. He was married twice, and had Marie-Thérèse Walter as a life partner for more than 40 years, until his death at 91. Throughout his life Picasso maintained a number of mistresses in addition to his wife or live-in partner. At 61 years old, initiating an affair with Françoise Gilot that lasted six years, he told the then-21-year-old, "For me there are only two kinds of women, goddesses and doormats." I don't know what Picasso, who is often accused of being a misogynist, meant by this statement. But I laud him for his provocative delivery of a great wisdom.

The purpose of a doormat is to clean the sole of your shoes. A doormat exists to be stepped on, which is why the term is used to describe people who let others "walk all over them"; perpetual victims who seldom stand up for themselves. Life happens to a doormat. A goddess, on the other hand, is a deity. The word evokes images of powerful women, beauty, adoration, a clear sense of self, the antithesis of a doormat. Goddesses and doormats are polar opposites, so extreme that they could not possibly be the only two modes in which women operate, right?

Wrong.

I agree with Señor Picasso. You are either happening to life – being a goddess – or life is walking all over you – being a doormat. You are either the victim of people and circumstances or the mistress of your destiny. There are no in-betweens. Yes, we vacillate between the two. In one situation we may choose goddesshood, in another victimhood. Often victimhood is attractive because if things are happening to us, we can blame, elicit pity and wait for rescue. Victimhood is easy, but it is disempowering. Opting instead to be a goddess requires taking responsibility for your life and everything in it – your happiness, financial situation, health, career, relationship satisfaction, everything. It's a scary idea, but it is extremely empowering.

The gift of responsibility is freedom and power, core attributes of a goddess. Before you can change anything you must take responsibility for it. Most of us translate "responsibility" as "your fault". Responsibility is not about blame; it is about empowerment. It gives you the ability to respond. To change something, you must first accept responsibility. If you are a victim and stuff is happening to you, you cannot affect the situation in any significant way; all you can do is react to it – which brings us to another important distinction, the difference between reacting and responding.

Reacting is automatic, responding deliberate. Reaction occurs without conscious thought, often in emotional situations where we need deliberation the most. Our brains are wired in such a way that we automatically react to emotional situations. The oldest part of our brain, made up of the limbic system and amygdala, springs into action without engaging our neocortex, the part of the brain we use for rational thought. When we are confronted by an emotional situation, our old brain decides how to react, based on past experience and old, stored, judgements. Unfortunately, our old mental files are not always appropriate in new situations. If you keep on reacting instead of responding, you continue to recreate the past, since your reactions are based on it.

My mother is notoriously tardy; punctuality is like Kryptonite to her. As a child I lived with my maternal grandparents and my life revolved around my mother's visits, usually on Saturdays. On the phone, prior to her visits, she would promise to come as early as possible on the Saturday morning so we could do all sorts of things together. More often than not she would arrive only in the afternoon. I would wake up at the crack of dawn, wash, get dressed and wait. Since she always promised me that this time she would be on time, I'd work myself up into a complete frenzy from worry, convinced that her current delay was due to some horrible fate that had befallen her. This is what is filed in my brain under "waiting". As a result, I do not react well to waiting. My friends, family and colleagues can attest to this. I've left colleagues to find their own way to the airport and I've been known to call off a date because of being so upset by waiting that my mood was completely non-conducive to going out. Probably because of my issue with waiting, I am freakishly punctual. Even when I try to be late I still arrive before everyone else, and consequently spend a lot of time waiting for people. The irony is not lost on me. If I had continued to react to waiting I'd have emotional meltdowns on a weekly basis, so I had to learn to respond to waiting. Now I plan for it. As soon as the person I am expecting fails to arrive on time, I call to find out how long the delay will be. The people in my life know to tell me the truth, not to give the ubiquitous "I am five minutes away" line, often uttered by someone still in their pyjamas. This helps me to manage my expectations. I live in Johannesburg, an evil junction between horrendous traffic and fabulous people who must be "fashionably late", so I do a lot of waiting. I have turned my waiting time into email time. I always have a laptop, smartphone or iPad with me, so I can be productively occupied while I wait. It works so well that sometimes I hope to be kept waiting just so I can get through my emails.

This is a small matter in which I choose goddesshood over victimhood. This choice has given me control over a minor aspect of life, but the power of this choice is best appreciated in the big things. This is well illustrated by two young women I encountered a week apart. The first one, Lerato, was struggling with a drug abuse issue. When I met her, she had been using drugs for almost a decade and they were clearly taking their toll. She was raised by her mom – her dad having been absent until she was 13 years old, at which point he decided to establish a relationship with her. He would visit during school holidays and they spent a lot of time getting to know each other. They got on fabulously and her dad promised to become an active part of her life. Not long after, he was shot dead. Lerato sought solace in drugs. This became her habitual reaction to emotional pain. Soon after my conversation with her, I attended a talk by a young woman who was also in her early twenties; a professional motivational speaker and youth leader. Her choice of career was a response to her parents' death from AIDS when she was in primary school, which turned her into an AIDS orphan at a time when the stigma around the illness was at its peak. As she was rejected by relatives who didn't want to be tainted by her parents' scandalous deaths, she had to grow up very quickly. This sensitised her to the support and guidance children require from adults – resulting in her choice of vocation. These two women had rough childhoods. One became the victim of her fate; the other the mistress of her destiny. This statement by Judah Isvaran[3] feels to me like the "better" half of Picasso's pithy goddesses and doormats declaration: "Every day as you awake, you have a choice to place a crown upon your head and heart or to place shackles upon your Being. Your consciousness determines which you will choose. King/Queen or Slave. The cynical scowl, complain, bitch and blame... the powerful engage, create, inspire and give. All a choice... The World owes you nothing. Show Up. Wear your Crown." It may be easier to choose victimhood, but something amazing happens to you when you choose respond-ability, you get to happen to your life. You get to be powerful. Martin Luther King defined power as the ability to effect change. Power is not a dirty word, Evie. This is why you want to be powerful, so you can effect change in your world.

Thank goddess for bootcamp.

Becoming a Goddess: Empowering Yourself

8. Learn to Respond: In your journal, write out a scenario in which you habitually react to circumstances. Write it out as it typically unfolds. Think of a way in which you'd prefer to respond to it. Write that out in the present or past tense. Read it repeatedly, preferably out loud, until the idea of responding in the new manner does not feel foreign to you. You will have access to the new response, instead of only the usual reaction, next time you are faced with a similar situation.

9. Choose Goddesshood.
   a. List in your journal all the areas in your life where you appear to have chosen victimhood.
   b. Play the "what if?" game with them. "What if I were to take responsibility in this situation, how would I change it or myself?"
   c. Take the least daunting situation and test-drive your goddesshood on it. As you build confidence, go through your entire list.

10. Watch the movie *What the Bleep Do We Know*. It gives concrete scientific proof that you are indeed the centre of your universe. It will give you a great excuse to act as if the world revolves around you.

11. Divine Inspiration: If you struggle from "doormatitis", you really must meet Lilith, a member of our goddess bootcamp crew, page 235.

The Caterpillar and Alice looked at each other for some time in silence: at last the Caterpillar took the hookah out of its mouth, and addressed her in a languid, sleepy voice.
"Who are YOU?" said the Caterpillar

This was not an encouraging opening for a conversation. Alice replied, rather shyly, "I – I hardly know, sir, just at present – at least I know who I WAS when I got up this morning, but I think I must have changed several times since then."

"What do you mean by that?" said the Caterpillar sternly. "Explain yourself!"

"I can't explain myself, I'm afraid, sir," said Alice, "because I'm not myself, you see."

Excerpt from *Alice's Adventures in Wonderland*
by Lewis Carroll

Know Thyself

One of the most courageous things you can do is identify yourself, know who you are, what you believe in and where you want to go.

~ Sheila Murray Bethel

Whose life are you living, Evie?

The word "Veritas" is tattooed on my wrist. *Veritas* is Latin for truth. I inked it there after making a disturbing discovery about my life. One lazy Sunday afternoon, I was reading a magazine article about goals, in which it was suggested that I write down my top 10 goals for the new year, in order of priority, and put them in a place where I'd see them often enough for them to direct my daily actions. I did – 10 goals, in order of priority. Then I had a curious thought. What if other people could not approve or disapprove of me, what would my list look like then? I pondered this question for a while, then decided to play pretend, imagining that I lived in a world where people could neither approve nor disapprove of me. I wrote down a new list, based on this fictional approval-free world. Most of us are not immune to coveting the approval and avoiding the disapproval of others. For instance you may plan to quit smoking, not because you want to, but because you know your loved ones hate your habit.

When I compared my new list to the original, there were differences. Two goals had been replaced and I had changed the priority of a few others. I did some more pondering on what this meant, when that voice piped up again, "Wow, so this is the power approval exerts over you! Have you been designing your life around the approval of others all this time?"

I was having a mini freak out when the voice surfaced once more. It was on a roll. "What would you pursue in a world completely devoid of approval by others or yourself?" Now, Evelet, you know that you often give or withhold approval from yourself – like when you break your diet, convince yourself that shopping is exercise or spend half the day on the internet.

I took a fresh piece of paper and imagined a world completely devoid of the concept of (dis)approval, not only by others but also by myself. I wrote a new list, 10 short-term goals in order of priority. In comparing this new list with the one before, I realised I had replaced three goals and promoted another two. There were small differences between the original list and the second list, as there were between the second and third lists, but what was shocking was the difference between the first and third lists. Only half the goals in list one featured in the last list and the order of priority was completely different. Whose life was I leading? Who were these people whose approval I sought? What is the origin of my internal (dis)approval dispensary? Whose voices had colonised my mind?

We all have regular flashes of insight – "Aha! Moments", as popularised by Oprah after Jean Shinoda Bolen coined the phrase. The problem is that if we don't anchor the insight quickly its energy dissipates. Soon, all we have is a vague memory of having glimpsed the light. This particular Aha! Moment had shaken me so profoundly that I was unwilling to lose it. The following day, at lunch time, I popped into the tattoo studio and had "Veritas" inked on my left wrist. It is my shorthand from Shakespeare's *Hamlet* – Polonius's last piece of advice to his son, Laertes, as he is about to leave for Paris, "This above all: to thine own self be true."

To be true to yourself, you have got to know yourself. How else will you judge your fidelity to self? Years ago, one of the major cellphone companies had an ad I loved that played with the word "freedom". It had a crazed-looking Trevor Gumbi reciting a promotion for an airtime package through prose. It ended with the question, "Are you free or are you *dom*?" I loved that. I am a word junkie, I love scrabble and do crosswords with a pen. Yep, I am a word nerd. I notice many things about words; their meanings, origins, make up and relationship, but I'd never picked up that the word freedom had the English word "free" and the Afrikaans word "*dom*". Are you free or are you *dom*? This genius line got me thinking about free will, or rather the illusion of free will.

Free will is central to many people's identity as human beings. There is a widely held belief that humans have free will. This is supposedly what differentiates us from the animal kingdom and proves our superiority. We get to choose our actions, while the actions of animals are wired into them. That is what makes them *dom* and us free – the fact that we have free will. But do we really? In my view, the average person is far from free. We may not be governed entirely by instinct, like animals are, but we are governed by conditioning. We tend towards the choices programmed into us, like robots. Since most of us are unaware that our choices are dictated by our conditioning, we have an illusion of free will. Which makes us *dom*. We are conditioned from infanthood. We call this conditioning by many names: socialisation, upbringing, manners, education and culture. When we are young our parents, caregivers, teachers, siblings, peers, environment and the media tell us what is right and wrong, what we should and shouldn't do, what we should and shouldn't want, what is acceptable and what is not, what will gain us love and approval and what will get us rejected. All this dictates the kinds of intention, dreams and aspirations we should have.

For years, I was anti-marriage and never really questioned why. One day a group of girl friends and I were chatting about childhood fantasies. I was the only one who had no recollection of having had wedding fantasies. When I fantasised about adulthood it was often about independence, having a drawer full of frilly lingerie and being free not to wash dishes. I wanted to grow up to be a free, non-dishwasher in hot panties. I bet a shrink would have a field day with that. I became curious about why I never had this, seemingly common, girlhood wedding fantasy. Then I recalled that my mother, who upon reflection is really not built for traditional marriage, would often tell me how lucky I was to have been born during an age when I didn't have to get married. This always gave me the impression that I was incredibly fortunate to have the choice to escape the curse of marriage. She never said I shouldn't get married, or that marriage sucked, but her message was clear: you have the enviable opportunity to choose not to get married. So I did just that, at a very young age I chose not to want marriage, but it was never an informed choice. I just did as my mother suggested.

In high school, a friend convinced herself that she didn't want to have kids because of what a fortune-teller said. There was a gypsy carnival in town and she went to have her future divined from a crystal ball by an old gypsy woman with red talons, giant hoop earrings and a smoker's cough. The seer told my friend that she wouldn't be able to have children. She was devastated. Years later we were flat mates in our early twenties and one day she mentioned that she didn't, and never had, wanted children. She did not appear to remember the high school incident with the gypsy woman, but I did. She had somehow convinced herself that she had chosen childlessness. Luckily, the last time I saw her, she was a very happy mother of two.

As we get older, our programming comes from more impersonal sources, such as the books we read, the movies we watch and the songs we hear. They all colour what we think and expect from important things like life, people and love. Although I am a qualified and experienced marketer, I never truly appreciated media influence until I found myself bottom-half naked in a stark white cubicle, getting a Brazilian wax. Having pubic hair was perfectly acceptable, then one day it wasn't, and I couldn't even identify the tipping point. If you are exposed to a message often enough it takes root in your brain and lodges itself firmly without you even noticing. Repetition is insidious. That is how both advertising and propaganda work, through repeated exposure to a certain message. Ads tell us what we should want and how we should look. The news tells us how we should feel, who and what we should be afraid of, and who we should love or hate. Movies show us what we should strive for, how real love appears, the right level of bling for an engagement ring and how an orgasm should look. Whoever owns the media gets to control our minds. Anyone plotting a decent coup knows this, and few places are as colonised as our minds.

Evelet, I bet you don't like the idea that you are merely a flesh robot acting out your programming, but even the language we use is telling. When faced with questions of values and morals we say things like, "I was brought up to believe...", "My mother always said...", "Where I come from...". Implying that had we been raised by other people, elsewhere, we would choose differently. Religion is a great example of this; most people believe in, practice and identify with the religion they were born into. In South Africa, if you are black and religious, chances are that you are Christian. But had you been born white in Israel you'd most probably be Jewish, or had you been born brown in the Middle East then you'd most likely be Muslim. So the final destination of many souls was predetermined by geography. Meaning, where you end up depends entirely on where you started. It's all about location, location, location, it seems.

All these beliefs, which came into our lives as advice, manners, warnings, admonishments, compliments, fairy tales, songs, and religious teachings, govern our behaviour, our choices. Yet very few of us stop to question them, despite the fact that it's through choices that we create our lives. We hardly ever ask, Is this true? Is this true for me? Is it true that love hurts? Is it true that all good things come to an end? Is it true that hard work pays off? Is it true that God prefers poor people? Is it true that all men are only after one thing? Why must work come before play? Why can't you have it all? Why must I put my children first?

We hardly ever question our beliefs, despite the fact that most, if not all, of them were inherited from someone else. I am a keen gardener with a big problem. I am deathly afraid of the usual citizens of the garden: worms, caterpillars, snails and slugs. This makes gardening a tricky activity for me. There is a lot of screaming, running and shuddering involved. I fear the slimies because my grandmother fears them. She is an avid gardener and when I was a kid I would potter about the garden with her, which is probably why I love gardening in the first place. Just as I do now, she'd scream and bolt every time she encountered an earthworm. This is a cute fear to inherit, but don't let that distract you from the insight; we even inherit our loves and fears.

We do have free will because we are always free to change our beliefs. But most of us never even examine why we believe the things we do; let alone contemplate choosing differently. Instead, we merely live out our programming. Our lives are built by our choices and actions, which in turn are governed by our beliefs. Become curious about yourself, your reactions, your beliefs, your likes and dislikes. Where do they come from? Are you happy with them? Don't be scared to ask yourself these questions, because if you don't like them, you can change them.

If you have done all the "right" things – got the right education, in the right career, married to the right man, drop the right names, moulded your body into the right shape, have the right address – and you still feel like something is not quite right, perhaps what is wrong is the life you are leading. It may not be yours, but one belonging to the voices in and around you. A Facebook friend of mine had an insightful status once: "If they hold a 10-year reunion at my high school next year, I have less than one year to acquire a husband, 2.1 kids, a German sedan and a 4x4 parked in the right neighbourhood." I gather from her tongue-in-cheek tone that she recognised this was what she was expected to strive for, but that she is not necessarily buying into it. There is nothing wrong with any of these things, but they are not everyone's cup of tea. Sadly, most people never allow themselves the opportunity to examine if they truly want what they've been programmed to acquire. In such situations, success can be more devastating than failure. If you get it all and you feel empty it often aches more than if you are still striving for it all.

In *The Seven Spiritual Laws of Success*,[4] Deepak Chopra defines success as the continued expansion of happiness and the progressive realisation of worthy goals. Absolutely no one can define that for you, Evie. Know thyself and once you do, be true to yourself. You can only live a life of WOWness if it is your life, the life your true heart desires.

Becoming a Goddess: Discovering Your True Self

12. Redefine your definition of success to be 100 per cent personalised for you.
    a. Write a story in your journal of the ideal day in your life. In fact do two, an ideal weekday and an ideal weekend. Write them in the present tense. What time would you wake up? Is someone lying next to you in bed; if so, who? Where are you? What do you do when you get up? Who else is in the house; any pets? Do you live alone or do you have a family, staff? Do you have somewhere to go, where? Do you work, if so, what do you do? What activities occupy this day, which people and places? You get my drift. Write out your ideal day in as much detail as possible.
    b. How far off is your current life from the life you wrote about?
    c. Read these two stories often, if you can, first thing in the morning and last thing at night.

   d. Make a vision board with images of this life and put it in
   a prominent place.

13. Pay attention to yourself, your thoughts, reactions, feelings
    and actions. Be curious about their origin. Are they in
    alignment with who you want to be?

14. Learn EFT – Emotional Freedom Technique. EFT is one of the
    most effective ways I have used to change old, limiting beliefs.
    It is very easy to learn and do. There are lots of websites on
    EFT, but best start with the original one from the founder, Gary
    Craig. www.emofree.com

15. Cut down on the amount of media you expose yourself to. If
    nothing else, remember that the people who are affecting the
    world hardly spend hours in front of the TV. It's the people
    who spend hours in front of the TV who are being affected.
    Remember players and spectators? You can always come
    up with an activity juicier than trying to keep up with the
    Kardashians.

16. Talk to the people who brought you up about their childhood.
    The more you get to know them the better you will understand
    why they imparted the particular lessons they transferred to
    you. Perhaps after that you may decide to choose a different
    truth for yourself.

17. Write on a fresh page of your journal, "I should…" Finish
    that sentence with as many things as you can think of that you
    should do. Then ask yourself, why? If you really wanted to
    do these things, wouldn't they be done already? What are you
    doing in your life that starts with "should"? Must you? What
    would you rather be doing?

18. Divine Inspiration: Ask Grecian moon goddess Artemis to help
    you be true to yourself.

Choose You

Don't compromise yourself. You're all you've got.

~ Janis Joplin

Who have you been choosing?

As you probably discovered in the previous session, finding yourself through the cacophony of competing internal and external voices is extremely difficult, scary and uncomfortable work. So when you do eventually find you, Evie, have the courage and conviction to choose you. You need courage to choose you, because we live in a society that not only rewards conformity, but often punishes non-conformity. People are generally uncomfortable with – even disapproving of – those who do their own thing.

I remember once having a catch-up session with a friend who I hadn't seen in a number of years. I was in a very good place at the time; she, on the other hand, was having a rough time in her marriage. After going on about how challenging marriage was proving to be, she asked, without a hint of irony, when I intended to get married. We had just established that I was very happy with the current state of my life, while she wasn't very satisfied with hers, the biggest thorn in her side being her marriage. Yet she still asked, without missing a beat, when I was going to get married! When I pointed this out to her, she justified it by saying that considering what I do at The Goddess Academy – I support, inspire and empower women to create lives they love – being married would be better for business because single women in their thirties seem like losers. Apparently the fact that I genuinely did love my life didn't carry much weight. After our conversation, I decided to run an online poll in which I asked people to pick a preferred state between two options: (1) you appear positively ecstatic with your life but you are in fact mildly dissatisfied with it, or (2) you appear extremely miserable with your life but in fact you are the happiest you have ever been. It turned out that most of those who responded would rather experience mild dissatisfaction but appear very happy, than be very happy and appear miserable.

In which tribe do you fall, Evelicious?

The results of that vote reminded me of a parable[5] I encountered while training to get my Imagine A Woman (IAW)[6] life coach certification:

In the dark of the night thieves entered a store and did their work without detection. In the morning the store opened at the appointed time. It was obvious to the clerk that the store had been entered, yet nothing seemed to have been taken. As the day progressed and customers brought merchandise to the counter, the storekeepers noticed a curious phenomenon. The merchandise of least value wore the tags of greatest value. And the items of greatest value carried the tags of least value. By the end of the day the puzzle had been solved. The thieves had reversed the price tags.

My friend, and the people I polled, seemed to have reversed the price tags.

There are evolutionary reasons that survival of the individual, as well as the group, requires conformity from individual members of the group. As a result, people are still, irrationally, averse to non-conformity – even when it is not a threat to physical survival.

Society is not very accepting of our varied distinctiveness. Often the unique self is criticised, judged and punished into submission and an artificial, constructed, self emerges. For instance, we learn soon enough that how you appear is more valuable than who you are or how you feel. There are numerous problems with this route we have chosen. It makes for a lonely world, full of miserable and discontented souls, wearing the masks of happy, shiny people.

Pretending to be happy requires that you cover yourself up with a fake persona. The price is so very high, Evelet. If you are not being yourself, you don't really have an opportunity to have a true connection with other people. Intimacy requires openness. It requires you to show up and say, "This is me."

To appear as if you are winning means that you have to be successful, based on society's standard. In my sphere, the standard definition of "having it all" is having a lot of money which you spend on things – a big house in the right suburb, designer clothes, a luxury car, preferably an SUV that only ever climbs mall pavements, a sleek convertible, or pricey German sedan, ridiculously expensive beauty habits, such as hair extensions worth R6 000, an exclusive private school for your kids, and overseas holidays. All this must be accompanied by an authoritative position for yourself – even if all you get to bully are your maid, gardener and kids' nanny – and a super high-powered position for your husband. Of course, you must also look a certain way, not only your clothes, but the actual shape and size of your body. What if you are happiest on a farm somewhere, away from faux Tuscan villas and shopping malls? What if you have never been interested in having 2.1 kids? What if doing what you love is a lot more important to you than earning a lot of money to buy things you don't need, to impress people you don't like? What if marriage does not appeal to you? If you are such a person, and you buy society's standard success package, you will be miserable at worst and, at the very least, extremely under-whelmed by life. If you don't buy into it, you'll appear to be a loser.

I know a lot of people who are miserable and confused. They

have sought and bagged the standard success package, but they are uninspired by their lives. They thought they were going for WOWness but ended up with "whatever". Some have never examined if they want for themselves what society wants for them, others are just not courageous enough to choose anything different, so they lead lives of quiet desperation, perfecting *looking* happy instead of *being* happy.

A big part of choosing yourself is about putting yourself first. When you put yourself first, especially as a female in a society that has made self-sacrifice a virtue for women, you will be branded as selfish. Imagine if we ignored the airline's safety procedure, which insists that in case of an emergency you must secure your own oxygen mask first before attending to anyone else who may need help. If we rushed to put oxygen masks on children, the elderly and the injured before we had our own oxygen supply we would soon pass out, creating an even bigger mess. Ironically this illogical way is how we tend to approach real life. We think it is noble to pour from an empty jug.

What is being selfish, really?

Often when someone brands you as selfish what they are really saying is that you are meeting your own needs instead of theirs, you are putting yourself ahead of them. They want to come first. Does that not make them selfish, too?

To put yourself first you are going to have to exercise your "No" muscle. It is very important to have boundaries that others cannot cross. I had a boss who violated people's boundaries all the time. He was a nice guy, but he would call, text and email after hours, on weekends, even while you were on leave. My entire corporate career has been in media and marketing. I have never worked in a life-or-death industry such as health, defence or even the UN, so technically no "emergency" in my work life has ever been a real emergency. No lives have ever been in jeopardy because I did not respond to an email on a Sunday afternoon. This guy made people so miserable that a few resigned because of his constant invasion and demands on their private time. I never understood why they would choose to leave jobs they otherwise liked rather than tell one guy to fall back. Fortunately for me, I received my lesson in boundaries early in my career. Fresh out of varsity I had a boss, a married man, who used to assign the extra work to the single and childless staff. He'd say, "Stay here and work. What are you going home to, your fridge?" It was normal for me to leave the office around midnight and work weekends. The worst part with such situations is that the harder you work the more work you are given. Other people become lazy because they know that you are there to pick up the slack. After that job, I learned to maintain very clear boundaries. In subsequent jobs, I had two cellphones: business and personal. When I was at home I'd keep my work phone in the cubbyhole of my car. When I first started working for the boundary transgressor, he would ask me on Mondays why I hadn't responded to his calls, texts or emails from the weekend and I would inform him, firmly and with no disrespect, that when I get home, I leave my work behind. It took a while to train him, but eventually he learned to respect my boundaries. You need to love yourself enough to say "No" to other people's demands on your time and energy. Learn to say "No" to those things that you do out of guilt, a misguided sense of obligation, the fear of being labelled as selfish and, here's the big one, the fear that people may discover that they actually don't need you. That's a scary one, hey Evie? When people discover that they don't need you, they may just leave you. Guess what? The best people to have in your life are the ones who want to be there, not the ones who need to be there.

Choosing yourself and being true to yourself requires a lot of courage. The bravest part is not charting your own path, putting yourself first, or establishing boundaries. It is allowing yourself to be seen as you truly are and accepting that you may not be everyone's cup of tea; that some people won't appreciate or want you. There will be rejection. Try very hard not to abandon yourself to win the acceptance of others. I sometimes catch myself trying to fit into someone else's idea of what I should be – and often it is people whose opinion doesn't even matter to me. I discovered that my trigger is when someone says "that is so unlike you". I immediately want to backtrack and justify my actions or explain that they were an aberration that won't happen again. The fascinating part is that people who say something is "unlike you" are often those who don't know you very well. They have painted you in a single hue and are not interested in accommodating your kaleidoscope of colours. Generally, the people who really know you understand that sometimes you are a solid brown and at other times you are like a peacock. However, most of us are terrified of rejection and, if we could, we'd choose to be accepted by everyone. Fortunately, that is an impossible task, so stop bothering. In her book *The Gifts of Imperfection*,[7] professor and researcher Brené Brown, says she wishes that people came with a warning label stating, "Caution: If you trade in your authenticity for safety, you may experience the following: anxiety, depression, eating disorders, addiction, rage, blame, resentment, and inexplicable grief." Bootcamp baby, I didn't say it was going to be easy, but it is simple.

Choose you.

Becoming a Goddess: Choosing You

19. If you didn't write your own version of success as suggested in the previous session, this is your chance. What do you really want? Forget what everyone else says you should want. What do *you* want? What expands your heart and fills you with peace, joy and excitement?

20. Why don't you have what you want? Who or what is standing in your way? Whose rejection or judgement do you fear?

21. In which ways have you been abandoning yourself for the acceptance or comfort of others?

22. How can you start choosing you? Write all this down in your journal and commit to it.

23. Divine Inspiration: Look to Babylonian goddess Ishtar to help you maintain boundaries and Kali to give you courage to choose yourself.

Change Only You

We do not see things as they are, we see them as
we are.

~ Anaïs Nin

Are you itching for change yet?

After the first few sessions you may be inspired to start making
some changes in your life. Perhaps you'd like to trade in the
standard success package for a bespoke ideal. In that case, well
done to you, Evelet! Go for it, but I must caution you: in your
metamorphosis, change only you.

When we are dissatisfied we look for something to change,
which is good, but usually that something tends to be someone –
which is not so good, or effective for that matter. You know what
I mean. You acknowledge that your relationship has lost its spark
and conclude that is because your lover is not as attentive and
romantic as he used to be; if he would become more like he was

before, things would change for the better. Work is unbearable because you have an A-grade asshole for a boss; if she had the good grace to choke on her own puke and die your life would be perfect. You are a ball of frayed nerves because your children are unruly, your neighbours are loud, inbred imbeciles and the roads are filled with suicidal inglorious bastards. You get my drift. If all these people would just behave themselves, or die, half your problems would be gone, hey Evie?

Probably not.

In fact, no.

In this session of goddess bootcamp we are going to learn from an unlikely source: babies – chubby, toothless, leaky, adorable babies. To be more precise, babies eating lemons. Have you ever watched those YouTube videos of babies eating lemons? You must. It's a good laugh and, personally, I think we don't get enough opportunities to laugh at babies. Even better, if you have access to a baby – preferably not a tiny infant – give him a slice of lemon, which will undoubtedly go straight into his mouth. Babies don't expect that acidic tang and, when it hits the back of their tongues, their reactions are priceless. Their whole bodies go into spasm. Stay with me, Evie, there is a point to this exercise other than the torture of infant homo sapiens. The fascinating thing is not their reaction to the taste, albeit entertaining, but that they usually give the lemon another go, get the same bitter hit and still try again, and again!

Once, when talking to my mother about this curious phenomenon, she suggested that perhaps babies keep trying because they think they are doing it wrong and if they figure out how to suck it just right it will taste different. That is more than plausible because babies have open minds. They know there is a lot they still have to learn. You can see sheer determination to be better lemon eaters etched in their chubby faces as they go for another hard suck of their citric nemesis. Babies have an entirely different relationship to mistakes and failure. When a baby who is learning to walk stumbles and falls, she doesn't quit, feel angry, or ashamed. She integrates the lesson and quickly gets up for another attempt. In your quest to makeover your life, adopt the attitude of a lemon-sucking infant; assume that you are the reason your life tastes bitter.

This is the perfect point at which to introduce you to some Universal Laws, but first let me tell you what happened to me this morning. I got stuck on the roadside because my car ran out of petrol. I know! I was very annoyed with that stupid car. I wasn't about to call roadside assistance in such a lame predicament, so I decided to deal with it myself. I threatened to donate my car to the South African Black Taxi Association. Yep, I was playing dirty. You'd think the bloody thing would budge, but it still didn't start. I changed tactics and tried some emotional blackmail. I reminded it of the time I took it to get all its little dents removed, the damn thing still wouldn't start. Bribery was next; I offered to get it some mag wheels. None of it worked. Eventually I got some petrol, and what do you know? The car purred to life, like magic!

Everything has rules, whether you like it or not. Cars do not go without fuel. Men don't fall pregnant. Water makes you wet. Things fall down, not up. If you know, understand and play by the rules, you can save yourself a lot of time, heartache, frustration and suffering. It doesn't matter how much sulking, bribing, negotiating or whatever else you do, you cannot get a fish to live out of water. Hence it is in your interest to acquaint yourself with the Laws of the Universe, which are obviously about how things work in the universe. Here is a quick summary of the Universal Laws most relevant to the matter at hand – your makeover to a life of WOWness.

The Law of One
There is only one thing in this entire universe. We are all part of that one thing. We are all connected. Separation is an illusion. Quantum physics has ascertained that the building blocks of the universe, quanta, consist entirely of energy. Everything in this universe is made up of the same thing, energy. The universe is a single field of energy in which physical matter is just a slowed-down form of the energy – in the same way that steam, water and

ice are different forms of the same thing. Yep, you, that dodgy guy from accounts, and the mysterious thing growing at the back of your fridge are 100 per cent the same, just arranged differently.

The Law of Vibration
Everything in the universe is in a constant state of vibration. Every thought creates a vibration, which travels out into the universe. As your thoughts are sent out into the universe they collect energy vibrating at the identical frequency and bring to you circumstances and people who reside on the same frequency. The higher the vibration the more positive the circumstances or people you attract and, conversely, the lower the vibration the less palatable the people and circumstances you attract.

The Law of Attraction
Everything draws to itself that which is like it. Energy attracts energy of a similar vibration. You attract to you other energies, manifested as objects, people, situations and experiences, with a similar vibration to yours. The rate of your vibration is determined primarily by your thoughts. You have created your life and everything in it through your vibration (thoughts) – your job, health, bank balance, relationships, the whole nine yards. We attract the things we give our attention and energy to. What you think about, you will tend to bring about.

The Law of Reciprocity
Whatever we give, we get back – or we get what we give. So whatever you want more of, start giving it away. This is a weird one. In order to get what you want you must give it away. If you'd like more money, share the money you already have. If you'd like more love, give love. The concept of tithing works on the same principle: you give in order to get.

The Law of Correspondence
This is the law most crucial to our session. It teaches us "as above, so below; as within, so without". Your outer world is nothing

more than a reflection of your inner world. Your current reality is merely a mirror of what is going on within you. What you see is what you reflect. Please let that sink in. Nothing is as it appears; everything appears as you are.

If life is merely a reflection of you, then the only thing you should, and can, change is you. When you look in the mirror and you don't like how you look in a certain outfit, you don't expect the mirror to go and change clothes. *You* change and the reflection in the mirror reflects the change. That, my dear Evelet, is exactly how life works. Just like a mirror. You are a goddess; the universe literally rearranges itself to reflect you to you.

We live in a magical wonderland. The universe gives us infinite opportunities to truly know ourselves. It's like living inside a giant inverted mirror ball, no matter where you look, there you are. Or you could see the universe as a big hologram – a three-dimensional picture in which the entire 3D image can be found in any piece of the film. The whole is contained in every part. As Deepak Chopra puts it, "We are not in the world, but the world is within us". You are the microcosm and the universe is the macrocosm.

I once had a rollercoaster of a relationship that taught me a hell of a lot about myself – which, incidentally, is the primary purpose of relationships. Relating is nature's mirror. Through our relationships with others we get to see ourselves as we truly are. The more intimate the relationship, the clearer the image. The clearer the image, the more visible our flaws become. Remember the Law of Attraction? Like attracts like, so you attract things, situations and people who are like you. At any given point you will attract to you the person or situation that most accurately reflects you. Have you noticed that when you are in a bad mood, you come across more angry people than usual and when you are late all the traffic lights are red for you? Back to my rollercoaster affair: I fell head over heels in love with a guy who soon fell head over heels in love with a destructive drugs- and alcohol-fuelled lifestyle. I expended a huge amount of energy trying to get him to stop. One day, while I was driving, I switched on the radio in time to catch an off-colour joke about a troubled couple on a visit to a marriage counsellor. The counsellor asked the wife, "What's the problem?" She responded, "My husband suffers from premature ejaculation." The counsellor turned to her husband and inquired, "Is that true?" The husband replied, "Well, not exactly, she's the one that suffers, not me." The message could not have been clearer. The Universe had made its point. I was the one who was suffering, not him. If he did not enjoy his lifestyle he would have made an attempt to change it. I was the one with a problem and thus, change was my responsibility. Soon after that Aha! Moment, I discovered the Universal Law of Correspondence. You know what they say, "When the student is ready the master appears." I read a book by Debbie Ford called *The Dark Side of the Light Chasers*,[8] which explains this law really well. I got it, but what I couldn't fathom was how my boyfriend's behaviour was in any way a reflection of me. Then I realised that he refused to let go of something that was obviously bad for him, drugs and alcohol, and I, too, was hanging on to something that was obviously bad for me: him. He was hooked on drugs and I was hooked on him!

I've put extra effort into making the point that the only thing you can change is yourself because, in my experience, this is one of the hardest sessions of bootcamp. It is the Goddess vs Doormat issue. It is less daunting to attempt to makeover other people. Changing yourself is scary and hard, so people just don't warm up to this truth. As I cautioned before, Evelet, I never said reaching the land of WOWness was easy, just simple. If it were easy, everyone would be there.

Here is an inspirational tale on the feats you can achieve when you focus your desire for change in the right direction: inwards. Dr Ihaleakala Hew Len healed an entire ward of mentally ill criminals at the Hawaii State Hospital, using Ho'oponopono – an ancient Hawaiian practice of forgiveness and reconciliation. He cured his patients without seeing even one of them. Dr Len worked there for four years, during which time so many of the patients were healed and released that the few who remained were relocated and the ward for the criminally insane was closed down. He did this by focusing on healing himself. He would sit in his office going through the patients' files. As emotions came up: pain, anger, empathy, whatever, he took full responsibility for those emotions and worked on healing them in himself. As he put it, "I was simply healing the part of me that created them." That is what Ho'oponopono – which means "to make right" – is all about, taking responsibility for your creations. It says that anything you experience is your responsibility – all of it, without exception, because the world is your world. Not your fault, but your responsibility.

You are responsible for healing whatever or whoever appears to you as an issue. When you change, the reflection in the mirror changes. When you yell/blackmail/manipulate the reflection yells/blackmails/manipulates right back with equal vigour.

Does that make you feel excited or wary, Evelet? It turns out that you really are the centre of the universe.

So whatchu gon' do about it?

Becoming a Goddess: Changing from the Inside Out

24. Use the world mirror to heal. Note the qualities that annoy you in other people. Honestly seek and identify that quality within yourself. Find a way to accept that attribute in yourself and the quality will no longer bother you when you encounter it in others. Say, for example, you have a girlfriend who dates men for money and this behaviour really grates you. Ask yourself, "In which way do I prostitute myself?" Listen quietly to your intuition. An answer rises up and says, "Evie, you hate your job, you don't believe in what you do. You only work there for the money." That right there is how you too are prostituting yourself. Then you have one of two choices, both of which will have the same result. You can leave this job for one that is better aligned with your values, or you can forgive yourself for being a prostitute. Either way your friend's behaviour will stop bothering you. Perhaps you have an extremely unreliable partner. This is because you let

yourself down. Do you fall off your diet wagon by lunchtime on day one? Do you keep on postponing going to the gym despite promising yourself that you were going to start on Monday? As soon as you start being someone you can rely on, your partner will do one of two things (a) he will also become reliable to you, or (b) he will leave your life, to be replaced by reliable people.

25. Become your own source of everything
    a. Identify all the things that you feel you should be getting, from people or situations, that you are not getting and find a way to give them to yourself. I'll use an example I am pretty sure everyone can relate to: pining for love. You want love, but you are lonely so you cannot have love. All you can have is more loneliness. The universe gives it right back to you. In the form of creepy blind dates who prove to you that all the eligible playmates have been taken and you are going to die lonely and miserable, your hands smelling of KY jelly. Eventually you get bored with feeling sorry for yourself and you start enjoying yourself. You take advantage of being single and you start doing all the things that you missed doing when you were part of a twosome. You watch the movies you like, go to the places you like, eat what you like, fart in bed and generally start having a blast with your fine self. In other words, you start loving yourself. Now you are vibrating love energy and then what happens? The universe obliges and gives you love.
    b. Give away what you want. If you wish you had more friends, become friendly to others. If you wish your partner was more supportive of your choices, become more supportive of his choices. If you could really use a hug and some kind words, look for someone else with a similar need and give that person a hug and encouragement. Remember, you cannot have what you *want*; you can have only what you *are*. Wanting something means you don't have it – so you

get more of that "not having it". Giving something away means you have it. Give what you want.

26. You create your world with your thoughts, powered by your emotions and based on your beliefs. Here is an exercise you can do to find out what your (mostly) unconscious beliefs are. In your journal, write the story of your life, from birth to the present. Focus on whatever feels important. Leave it for a couple of days so you can read it with fresh eyes. Then look for patterns. For instance, say you notice that you are often betrayed. Ask yourself, what kind of belief would someone have to attract such betrayal into their life? Perhaps you believe that people cannot be trusted. I have a cousin who believes that you can't have it all, so when things are going well at work, at home and at the bank, she gets sick. When her health is perfect, her relationship is fabulous and she has no money issues, one of her kids starts acting up, and so on. Once you identify your limiting beliefs you can then use EFT, hypnosis, or other techniques you might know of, to change your beliefs.

27. Must Read: *A Little Light on the Spiritual Laws* by Diana Cooper, or other books on Universal Laws.

28. Good to Watch: *What the Bleep Do We Know?*

29. Divine Inspiration: Butterfly Maiden will be of invaluable help as you embrace change.

It's Not All You

To step outside of patriarchal thought means...
overcoming the deep-seated resistance within
ourselves toward accepting ourselves and our
knowledge as valid. It means getting rid of the great
men in our heads and substituting for them ourselves,
our sisters, our anonymous foremothers.

~ Gerda Lerner

What is wrong with you, Evie?

I know you have a ready answer to this question. Had I wanted
to ask you a difficult one I would have asked, "What is right
with you?" In the book *Reviving Ophelia: Saving the Selves of
Adolescent Girls*,[9] author Dr Mary Pipher, a clinical psychologist,
recommends that girls and young women explore their culture's
impact on their growth and development. I'd say all people,
irrespective of their gender, race or age, should examine how

prevailing culture impacts their sense of self. The influence of our culture cannot be escaped. None of us is immune to it; it poisons your being – physical, mental, emotional and spiritual. Awareness becomes your greatest antidote.

Write a list in your journal of all the things that are wrong with you. Really, stop now and do it. Here are a few things that are wrong with me:

1. I suck at small talk and usually end up with my foot firmly lodged in my mouth. I have, on more than one occasion, congratulated a woman on her pregnancy when, unfortunately, she turned out to be 100 per cent unfertilised. The last time I had such serious verbal diarrhoea that when the lady told me she wasn't pregnant, I argued with her. Can you imagine?

2. I LOVE words, but some of the words I love the most are swear words. This is bad because I have a young and impressionable child.

3. I scare a lot of men, even when I am not trying to.

4. I am bottom heavy. Not as much anymore, because I got a boob job. Yes, my body issues were severe enough for me to subject myself to expensive and painful cosmetic surgery.

5. I have Daddy issues.

6. I have commitment issues. "What do you mean I must vow to love him forever?" Even the idea of committing to a TV series makes me panic. "You mean I have to watch it every single Monday at 7.30 pm? Nooooooooooooooo!"

7. I hate that when I am nervous it shows. My voice gets shaky, I talk too fast, I wring my hands and my words come out wrong. I would love to appear more composed and unshakable.

8. I still get pimples at my age, which is not a good look.

These are the ones I managed to rattle off without putting any thought into it. I can happily commit my defects to the pages of this book because it is a book for women, and women engage in a quaint little ritual called wound bonding. We connect over wounds. We trade war stories. We bond by exchanging defects and misfortunes. This may be one of the reasons that our conversations are so much longer than men's. Men can only talk about last night's game for so long. Heck, men can only talk for so long, period. But us – we can share, dissect, analyse, compare, commiserate and judge each other's shortcomings for days, with great glee and enthusiasm.

The reason I want you to put in black and white all the things that are wrong with you is that I would like you to critically examine your beliefs regarding what is wrong with you. Are you too fat? Why are you too fat? What is too fat? Are you too fat according to health standards, or beauty standards? Is it the doctor or the magazine editor who led you to believe there's more of you than is necessary?

The UK's ITV conducted an experiment in which a hundred women were given a special device they had to click each time they had a negative thought about themselves. On average, the women clicked the device 36 times every day. Imagine that! If you are up 16 out of 24 hours it means a negative thought about yourself every half an hour. Imagine the damage you would do to someone's self-esteem if you criticised them every 26 minutes of their waking day.

Did you know that twice as many women as men suffer from clinical depression?[10]

For aeons, women across the globe have been victims of physical and emotional abuse – from foot binding performed on Chinese women well into the 20th century, female genital mutilation still practised in parts of Africa, the Middle East and Southeast Asia, the present day routine raping of women in South Africa and the rampant global trafficking of girls and women into prostitution, to punishments meted out to women under Sharia Law. The list goes on. Yet, even in instances where we are free, empowered and protected, we willingly mutilate and poison ourselves. Elective cosmetic surgery and the injection of toxins such as Botox are on an upward trajectory. The violence we are willing to inflict on our bodies for a particular ideal is frightening. According to Datamonitor,[11] the global industry in beauty, anti-ageing and weight-loss potions was worth $7 billion in 2011. Evelet, we spent seven billion dollars trying to make ourselves look "better".

More women than men are unhappy with their appearance, have elective cosmetic surgery, go for psychotherapy, suffer from eating disorders, and are afflicted with anxiety disorders.

This is partly because more women than men are on the "What's wrong with me?"[12] quest.

How is that list of defects coming along, Evelet?

Mine has, at various times in my life, driven me to psychotherapy, the gym, fad diets, dysfunctional relationships and cosmetic surgery. If all people got together and made a global list of their imagined defects by gender how much longer than the men's list do you think ours would be? Twice the length? 100 times longer? Even so, this question, "What's wrong with me?" is not part of our DNA. We were not born thinking that we were defective. Young girls do not expend an iota of energy trying to figure out what is wrong with their bodies, feelings or thoughts. In fact, they tend to be the opposite; they celebrate themselves. They wiggle their naked little bodies in the mirror, revelling in their beauty. They fully expect you to display their abstract works of art on the fridge for all to see. They know that they are fabulous. One day Miss B and I were taking our evening walk, when she tossed a rubber ball into the air and it went much higher than she expected. With the most gleeful expression on her face, she gave herself a big hug and said, "I am wonderful".

How do we regress from butterflies to caterpillars? This belief that we are defective is shaped over time, by critical words, images, experiences and expectations starting beyond conception. Young girls are exposed to common criticisms, such as, "Good girls don't act like that", "Nobody will be your friend if you insist on being like that", "Hey! What is wrong with you?" These critics usually mean well. I often catch myself trying to reshape Miss B so she can fit in better. But I have to remind myself that the road to hell is paved with good intentions.

In reality, not all our critics have good intentions. In 2007 the *Journal of Consumer Research* published a study that proved what marketers and advertisers have known for ages; there is a causal link between low self-esteem and materialism. The shittier you feel the more inclined you are to buy shit you don't need. Through media and advertising we are subtly made to feel inadequate and the recommended cure is retail therapy. Alongside articles on how to get rid of your cellulite, have better orgasms and cheat-proof your relationship are glossy ads for stuff you can buy to make yourself feel better about your cellulite, unremarkable sex life and cheating spouse; beautiful shoes, luxurious cosmetics, designer outfits, island getaways. "You suck, here's a flat screen TV to make it all better."

Riddle me this: why do magazines digitally alter the appearance of the models they feature in their pages? Early in my career I had a short stint as a production assistant for a large clothing retailer. I would go to photo shoots for catalogues and the inserts that go into newspapers. Gorgeous models would spend what seemed like hours getting their hair and make-up professionally done and then be photographed under the most flattering lighting, by experienced professionals. Rolls of film would be used and only the best pictures would be selected. These would then be scrutinised on a lightbox with a special magnifying glass to identify flaws – shadows under the eyes, a hint of cellulite, a sag in the upper arm, too much curve in the hip, a pimple. The pictures would then be digitally altered to make the model virtually flawless. This is the picture that you see in a magazine, when you drive past a billboard or page through a catalogue. That standard of beauty is not attainable, but we see it so often we've begun to think it is real. A very impressive 14-year-old, Julia Bluhm, from Maine in the US, launched an online petition asking *Seventeen* magazine to use non-airbrushed images, because she and her friends felt that the digitally altered images negatively affected their self-esteem. Of course the magazine pulled out its best spin doctors to firmly, but sleekly, put her in her corner, but I admire her spirit. Some countries in Europe, such as Norway and France, have proposed legislation to label altered photographs, because these unrealistic and extremely idealised images have been linked to eating disorders, body image dissatisfaction and self-esteem issues, even in children.

This industry is certainly fuelling our fixation with real and imagined defects, but it is not the original culprit. Remember the story of Eve that we addressed in our first bootcamp session? The root of the "what is wrong with me?" question could even lie there. In her book *Be Full of Yourself!*[13] Patricia Lynn Reilly points out that "they extend deep into the ground of Western civilisation and the origination of its intellectual, theological, philosophical and psychological thought and practice". For example, this is how Greek philosopher Aristotle described the biological differences between men and women:

> The fact is, the nature of man is more rounded off and complete...
> Hence woman is more compassionate than man, more easily moved to tears, at the same time is more jealous, more querulous, more apt to scold and to strike... more prone to despondency and less hopeful than the man... more false of speech, more shrinking, more difficult to rouse to action, and requires a smaller amount of nourishment.

Along with Plato and Socrates, Aristotle is one of the most important founding figures of Western philosophy.

As if it is not enough for Aristotle to assert that we are jealous, complaining liars by nature he also wants to starve us: "requires a smaller amount of nourishment". I don't know about you but when operating on a calorie deficit, I could bite Aristotle's misogynistic head off without breaking my stride.

The Old Testament of the Bible also comes in handy in "proving" that women are inferior and defective. This is how 1 Corinthians 14: 43–35 reads in the King James version:

> Let your women keep silence in the churches: for it is not permitted unto them to speak; but they are commanded to be under obedience as also with saith the law. And if they learn anything, let them ask their husbands at home: for it is a shame for women to speak in the church.

It is a shame for women to speak in church. A shame.

Philo of Alexandria, a Hellenistic Jewish Biblical philosopher, penned a book entitled *Questions and Answers on Genesis*, in which he gave four reasons why woman was formed from man's rib and not from the earth like man and the other animals. Here are his justifications for women's second-class citizenship:

1. Woman is not equal in honour to the man.
2. She is not equal in age but younger. Wherefore those who take wives who have passed their prime are to be criticised for destroying the laws of nature.
3. He wishes that a man should take care of the woman as a necessary part of him: but the woman, in return should serve him as a whole.
4. He counsels man figuratively, to take care of the woman as of a daughter, and woman to honour the man as a father...

A man who takes an older woman as a wife must be shamed. Don't you just love that? Could such teachings be the source of the infantilisation of women? Society, the media – and especially fashion – prefer portrayals of women as little girls, lacking in power, will and maturity. Just the way old Philo insists the Bible likes it. I can just see old Philo slapping a very young Mrs Philo on the bum with an oily "who's your daddy?"

Adult women have bodily hair, on our arms, legs, armpits and genitals, but for decades we have been waging war against our body hair. Increasingly, hair can no longer take refuge on the genitals. First it was the bikini wax – just trimming the sides, then it was the Brazilian – where you leave a patch of hair or "landing strip" in the middle, and now the Hollywood where all the hair is removed, front all the way to the back, leaving you looking like a freshly plucked prepubescent. Adult women are trying to look like girls and young women are terrified of ageing. Many women in their twenties are getting preventative Botox injections. There is a video on the internet of a beautician giving her eight-year-old daughter Botox injections. This case is extreme enough to cause consternation, but the infantilisation soup we are marinating in is mostly subtle enough not to raise much ire. Ten years ago, would you have subjected yourself to a Hollywood wax?

For as long as I can remember, a particular beauty house has been preparing me to be able to spot the seven signs of ageing, so I could vanquish them before I start looking anything older than 26. More recently, I have seen an ad in which a young black woman in her early twenties is peddling an anti-ageing cream. The ad warns against age spots already lurking under the skin that, according to the voice-over, are certain to surface with age unless they are obliterated now with this miracle cream. I have yet to see a black woman under 80 with age spots, and trust me any woman who makes it to 80 has more profound things to thank than wrinkle potions. The message is loud and clear: women are only valuable and desirable when they appear youthful.

This is a double-edged sword. You cannot infantilise femininity without sexualising girlhood. I am not entirely comfortable with getting ready for a DWA – dirty weekend away – by removing all my pubic hair. I don't think adult men should feel okay having sex with a woman who has no pubic hair. Children have bare genitals, not adults. Childlikeness has been sexualised. The December/January 2011 issue of French *Vogue* had a spread featuring little girls dressed as women, in make-up, bright red lipstick, stilettos, some lying on tiger skins and beds flanked by leopard print scatter cushions. Have you seen how sexy dolls have become? If you thought Barbie was a dodgy toy for prepubescent girls, the newer ones make Barbie look like a nun.

Sigmund Freud, the father of psychoanalysis, taught that women are psychologically scarred as young girls when they discover that boys have penises and they don't. According to Freud, the resultant envy of the penis retards our development and character so severely that only a lot of psychotherapy can heal us. Incidentally, there are far more women than men in therapy. Things that make you go, hmmm. Freud's views are not that different from Aristotle's who, thousands of years before, said, "The female is, as it were, a mutilated male, and the catamenia [menstruation] are semen, only not pure; for there is only one thing they have not in them, the principle of soul."

These are a few, of many, examples of how religious, philosophical and intellectual thought-leaders positioned women, in our collective conscious and unconscious mind, as wrong and less than. Evelet, consider that the reason you may think something is inherently wrong with you as a woman is because that is the mould you have been cast in for 6 000 years.

In the last session of bootcamp, I cautioned that in remodelling your life, you should change only you. I now tell you that it is not *all* you. Be especially sceptical of the voice that tells you that you are defective. Remember also that we live in the era of reality shows, which are edited, produced and scripted to high heaven. In this world where everything is digitally altered, it is hard for a normal person to feel adequate.

Daughter of Eve, there is nothing wrong with you.

Becoming A Goddess: Releasing Your Imaginary Defects

30. Decide that you are blessed, not cursed. Write in your journal 25 reasons why it's great that you are a woman. I don't expect you to get to 25 in one sitting, but do commit to a minimum of 25. Once you get to 25 post them somewhere public, in your office, a blog or on The Goddess Academy Facebook group.

31. Identify all the things that make you feel inadequate and go on a 40-day detox from them. Apply a critical eye to the magazines you choose to read. Pay attention to whether you feel better or worse about yourself after reading them. Consider withdrawing your patronage from those that make you feel that you need fixing. The same applies to TV shows and people.

32. For 40 days, do nothing that is motivated by your belief that something is wrong with you. If you apply make-up not to enhance your beauty but to hide your flaws, for 40 days just stop. If you go to gym not to feel healthy and energetic but to get rid of "the junk in your trunk" just stop. Invest all that money, time and energy you usually use to keep your wrongness at bay in helping people with real problems. It will be good for you and them.

33. I love posting pre and post Photoshop pictures of famous celebrities on The Goddess Academy Blog and Facebook group to remind women that no one looks like the images that we are bombarded with on a daily basis. Do a regular Google search of these images until you get a healthy appreciation of what a real woman looks like.

34. Write a list of your defects. Examine how many of them are really yours. Use techniques such as EFT to help you release these limiting beliefs. Hypnosis also works very well for some people. Personally it does nothing for me, but I also know lots of people who have sworn by it.

35. Divine Inspiration: One of the things that made Aphrodite attractive was the fact that she was really comfortable in her own skin. She loved herself. Whenever you have thoughts about your imaginary defects, invoke your inner Aphrodite.

I will not die an unlived life
I will not live in fear of falling or catching fire.

I choose to inhabit my days,
to allow my living to open me,
to make me less afraid,
more accessible;
to loosen my heart until it becomes a wing, a torch, a promise.

I choose to risk my significance,
to live so that which came to me as a seed
goes to the next as blossom,
and that which came to me as blossom,
goes on as fruit.

by Dawna Markova

Free Your Heart

The best and most beautiful things in the world cannot be seen or even touched. They must be felt with the heart.

~ Helen Keller

How do you feel, Evelicious?

Do you feel freely with abandon or fearfully with restraint?

In our culture thoughts have been elevated over emotions. We have made thinking superior to feeling, in part because men are not as good at feeling as women are, but mainly because all of us, male and female, are afraid to feel. Emotions make us vulnerable, and few people willingly embrace vulnerability. We resist bad-feeling emotions because we are terrified that they will last forever. We resist good-feeling emotions because we are scared they won't last. In reality emotions are neither constant nor permanent. They are like waves, ebbing and flowing. Sometimes they're like massive tsunamis, threatening to wreck our lives, leaving only debris and casualties behind, at other times barely perceptible. Big or small, good or bad, they all eventually retreat. Instead of letting them be, we try to hang on to the good ones long past their sell-by date, and attempt to minimise the less pleasant ones.

The problem with suppressing emotions is that their very nature makes it futile. Emotion, e-motion, is energy in motion. Energy cannot be destroyed. It can only be transformed. The same way you can transform H_20 into a gas (steam), or a liquid (water), or a solid (ice), but you can't make it go away. By its very nature, energy flows. When it stops moving it stagnates and turns into something else, usually unpleasant. What it never, ever does is go away. It cannot be destroyed.

In childhood we learn to suppress emotions, hoping they will go away. Life is rough at times, even when you are a kid, perhaps especially when you are a kid. You feel sad, afraid, lonely, angry, rejected, frustrated, helpless, ashamed and vulnerable. Alas, from a young age, we are taught to be emotionally dishonest, and are rewarded for it; we disown emotions by suppressing them. Boys are taught not to cry, girls are taught not to be angry. We grow up rejecting certain emotions because of our conditioning, others we choose to suppress because they feel just too big to handle. For instance, a child experiencing abuse will often disassociate from her emotions due to their sheer magnitude. Either way, we think we have made the emotions go away by suppressing them, but what we have done is just put them below the radar of our conscious mind. Eventually they transform into what psychologists call personas or inner children. Now these inner children have an annoying habit of making cameo appearances at the most inappropriate times. We've all had those moments where we are just absolutely flabbergasted by our reactions, but at the same time feel powerless to stop them. This usually occurs when a person or situation triggers what Eckhart Tolle[14] calls our pain-body. An inner child just pops up and takes over, seemingly out of nowhere. I have watched myself in horror while acting as if I've been possessed by a needy six-year-old, with little ability to stop myself in that moment.

The pain-body is an accumulation of old emotional pain, usually from childhood, that we carry around with us in our emotional body. Very few of our emotional wounds are acquired in adulthood. Often, when we think someone or something has caused us pain, it is because they have triggered our pain-body. This happens often in intimate relationships and, for this reason, many people avoid relationships. A rare minority avoids relationships by not participating in them at all. The rest of us are less brazen – we have relationships, but we are not fully open and present in them for fear of getting hurt. Relating is nature's mirror and the closer a mirror the clearer we are reflected in it. As a result, our most intimate relationships have the greatest potential to reveal us to ourselves. The people we are closest to give us an opportunity to see the wounds in our energetic bodies, the fears and insecurities that restrain us. Sadly, we tend to assume they are inflicting the wounds when they are merely reflecting them back to us. Imagine that someone grabs your arm; if it's a healthy arm all you will sense is the pressure of the grip. If you have a gaping wound on the arm you will feel pain. That person, however, did not wound you; they merely touched you where you were already wounded. Perhaps it was a wound you didn't even know you had, providing you with an opportunity to heal it and expand your world. Instead of looking at relationships as providing opportunities to heal, we devise ways of being in relationships without getting too close for anyone to touch us and thus trigger our wounds.

Have you ever declared that you'll never again love as much as you've loved a particular ex, because you were determined not to let anyone "hurt you" like that ever again? I have. I have even argued the merits of being with someone who loves you more than you love them. A friend of mine cites this as the secret to marital bliss. I think her husband is the fortunate one, not my friend who withholds love for an illusion of control. Yes, the more you allow one feeling in (such as love), the more vulnerable you become to all others (such as rejection and insecurity). But the converse also applies: the more you try to keep certain feelings out the more you keep them all out.

Not all of us make this decision – to feel less – consciously. I didn't actually realise that I had my heart on lockdown until I had a child. I think because Miss B was too new and adorable to hurt me in any of the ways that had led me to build a fortress around my heart, I let my guard down for her, and I love her with all I've got. To give and receive love freely once again was such a refreshing and precious experience, but even this "safe" love exposed me to other emotions I wasn't keen on, such as fear, inadequacy, vulnerability, confusion and neediness. You cannot cherry-pick which emotions to feel. You open your heart for the good feelings and the bad feelings sneak in. In our attempt to shut out pain, we keep out joy. In rejecting sadness, our ability to feel love goes with it. This presents us with a conundrum, Evelet. What to do?

I vote for feeling. A lot of your power, especially as a woman, lies in your heart. If your heart is protected by walls, crowned with barbed wire and surrounded by a crocodile-infested moat, you cannot discern its guidance. In a TEDx[15] Talk he gave on the Intelligence of the Heart, Howard Martin[16] of the Institute of HeartMath[17] listed the following as some of the qualities of the heart:

• It is the source of wisdom and intelligence within us.
• It is the place from which our authentic self emerges.
• It is that place that we access when we are able to do what we usually can't.
• It gives us the ability to overcome obstacles.
• It fosters a deeper connection with ourselves and others.
• The heart gives us greater discernment and access to our intuition.
• The heart is our most reliable guide when it comes to making decisions.

In numbing our emotions, we lose out on all this.

How do you numb your emotions, Evie?

If you want a clue to how you anaesthetise your heart, look to your addictions. Addictions are a way we compulsively and chronically numb our emotions. One thing you've got to love about humans is our creativity when it comes to self-medicating.

We ignorantly assume that only drug addicts, alcoholics and compulsive gamblers have addictions, whereas we are hooked on food, work, shopping, drama, sex, exercise, the internet, rescuing others, surgery, worrying, planning, perfectionism, television – pretty much anything we can use to make us feel less vulnerable or distract us from our selves. Remember that American woman, the "Octomom", who was hooked on making babies? If it stops you from being present – here, with yourself, with others, with the world – and you "use" it routinely, then that, whatever that is, is your anaesthetic to feeling. You have to learn to tolerate, even welcome, vulnerability. There is no way that you can be truly you, and truly present, without being vulnerable. Otherwise you are relating through masks and walls and tricks and nobody ever gets to see the real you. And because you are beautiful, unique and unrepeatable, Evie, that's a heck of a pity.

How often have you overridden your feelings in favour of rational thought and later regretted it? We have all said "and I had a feeling about this", often too late. Feel more, feel deeper, feel often. Respect what you feel. For women, especially because we have greater feeling capacity than men, relying only on your mind to navigate through life is like choosing to use your left hand exclusively despite being right-handed.

Aren't you reading this book because you want to create a fabulously juicy life of WOWness? Why would you go to all this trouble if you were not planning on truly experiencing this life? It's like saving up for a fabulous beach holiday, then refusing to leave the room once you get to the island paradise. You cannot truly enjoy life through your mind, Evie. It's through the heart and the body that we get to party.

Here is one other reason for you to commit to feeling. Your feelings are integral to manifesting your life of WOWness. Although – thanks to Oprah and *The Secret* – it is now widely accepted that we create our reality with our thoughts, most people aren't doing much with this information. I don't blame them because it is a very daunting task to try to control your thoughts. After all, we apparently have an average of 42 thoughts a minute. Try to monitor that, Evie, without winding up in a padded room. Remember the Universal Law of Vibration? That every thought creates a vibration, which travels out into the universe and attracts circumstances and people that reside on the same frequency – something like the radio tuning in to a station on a particular frequency. The higher the vibration the more positive the events or people you attract and the lower the vibration the more negative the people and events you attract. Imagine the kinds of songs and interviews that would be on Fuck My Life FM versus Life Tastes Good FM. So monitoring your thoughts – all 42 a minute – and raising their vibration is vital if you are to wilfully improve the quality of your life experience. Luckily there is an easier way. Just pay attention to how you feel. If you feel "bad", choose a thought that feels better. This way you raise your vibration without that entire tedious mind-monitoring stuff. It's like magic.

No matter how you look at it Evelet, you can't have a life of WOWness without freeing your heart.

Becoming a Goddess: Freeing Your Heart

36. Become more in touch with your emotions. Pick three times in the day, say 8.15 am, 12.45 pm and 7.30 pm, and set your phone alarm to go off daily at these times. When it does, stop and ask yourself, "How do I feel?" and just tune in to your emotions. Do this for as long as you need to. If you feel bad, you can choose to stay with that emotion or reach for a thought that will lead to a healthier emotion.

37. Practice heart-centred breathing. For 10 minutes each morning, sit up with your eyes closed and your hand on your heart so you can feel your heartbeat, and breathe. Take deep and deliberate breaths. As you breathe, imagine that you are breathing in and out of your heart. Once you have a good

rhythm going, imagine that you are smiling through your heart. You don't need to understand with your mind how to smile with your heart; just do it.

38. Learn to move quickly through bad-feeling emotions. One way is by exaggerating them. As soon as you have some time to yourself, instead of suppressing the incident and the emotions it elicited, or steeling yourself against them, allow yourself to feel those emotions. Say you were feeling stupid. Feel stupid. Pour petrol on your stupidity by thinking about all the times that you have done really stupid things and have felt stupid. Allow yourself to be a giant ball of stupidity. Before you know it those emotions, like a raging fire, will burn out. Drink a glass of water – really, water helps emotions to flow – and give yourself a big hug, really. The next time you think about the situation that triggered those feelings, it should have less or no emotional charge.

39. Open up physically. When you feel yourself closing up, breathe through the resistance. Literally will yourself to remain open, and ensure that your body is physically open; uncross your arms or legs and avoid a hunched-over posture that covers up your heart.

40. Win with feelings. In your conversations, especially with men, look for opportunities to swap the words "I think" with "I feel/I sense/I perceive". Instead of saying, "I think we should go with the yellow paint", say, "I feel we should go with the yellow paint". Instead of, "I think ACME is the best company for the job", say "My sense is that we should give the business to ACME". This is good for two reasons: (1) It will signal to yourself your new-found respect for emotions and (2) Men are less willing to challenge your emotions than your thinking, so you tend to get away with a lot more this way. Sneaky, I know.

41. Must read: *Dear Lover: A Woman's Guide to Enjoying Love's Deepest Bliss* by David Deida. This is a great book on how to remain open in relationships.

42. Divine Inspiration: Ask the Celtic sun goddess Sulis, to help you foster a better relationship with your emotions.

Feed Your Soul

I think it pisses God off if you walk by the color
Purple in a field somewhere and don't notice it.

~ Shug
Character from *The Color Purple* by Alice Walker

How do you go about the care and
feeding of your soul, Evelet?

Death revealed to me the nature of life about a decade and a
half ago, when I realised I am not my body. I was home for my
grandfather's funeral. There was some old lady – you know how
random relatives come out of the woodwork at funerals – who was
intent on making us view my grandfather's body. I had never seen
a dead person and I was not terribly keen on the idea. I went out
onto the balcony, partly to ease my fear-induced claustrophobia,
but mostly to connect with memories of *ntatemogolo*. We used to
spend countless hours on that same balcony, just the two of us,

singing along to Harry Belafonte and Bill Withers. I found one of my uncles there, pensive. We stood together in a shared, sad silence. Soon the old lady found us and marshalled us towards the bedroom where they were keeping *ntatemogolo*'s body. I meekly succumbed to her herding, like a lamb to slaughter. I went through the macabre ritual as quickly as I could before bolting back to the balcony where my uncle, who had somehow managed to evade the event, asked me what the experience had been like. I told him the truth – the implication of which only dawned on me as I was responding. This was an Aha! Moment. *Ntatemogolo* wasn't there. There was a coffin, there was a body inside with a bit of cotton wool peeking out of the mouth, but my grandfather was not there. My grandfather, it turned out, was not his body. As I was standing in that room, looking into the coffin, it became very clear to me that the body was vacant; my grandfather no longer occupied it. This had been his body, but it had not been him. He was not his body. I realised that I, too, was not my body. Somehow I knew that I was the thing that animated my body. With this realisation I lost my fear of death and discovered my soul.

My high school was pretty progressive; we were instructed on a wide range of religions. When a bunch of us thought we'd score a free period by claiming we were atheist, to avoid Religious Instruction class, they brought in someone to school us on the theory of evolution. Exposure to a range of beliefs made me realise that, for the most part, religions are subjective, man-made constructs, not immutable laws. I see religions as providing a service, a structured spirituality for those who require it. This freed me to create my own belief system, having found the one I'd been born into ill fitting. I'd struggled and given up on connecting with the image of the jolly, pot-bellied white grandfather in the sky. I started nurturing my soul my way. Nature became and remains my church. I have always been attracted to nature and I feel most grounded, open, expansive and alive when romping with Gaia. When I want to pray, I seek lush surroundings. My regular spot is a little park in Jukskei Park, with majestic trees and a waterfall. There I take off my shoes so I can make a tactile connection with the earth. I breathe deeply while imagining that I am breathing through the soles of my feet, imbibing the energy of the earth. Then I talk to God(dess), I listen, I receive. Another way I nurture my spirit is with new beings. Infants have an ability to gently pry me open. I literally feel my heart centre open and grow beyond my body, when I play with babies, puppies and kittens. My energetic armour just melts away and I become one with life. In these ways I forge a fulfilling relationship with my inner and outer Spirit. My spiritual journey echoes that of Shug, the character in *The Color Purple* who said, "My first step from the old white man was trees. Then air. Then birds. Then other people." I, too, often find God(dess) in other people.

Evie, do not fear having a bespoke spiritual practice. Occasionally I'll let someone talk me into going to church, and every single time I have the same experience. I get bored out of my skull. I have tried all sorts of churches – from structured, sedate ones such as the Roman Catholic and Anglican churches, to energetic, charismatic ones where yelling, testifying, crying and breaking out in tongues is encouraged. They move me not an inch. I have accepted that I am not a church person and I am fortunate that it was easy for me to design my own spiritual practice that truly does feed my soul. When I go to my nature church, I come back feeling like I got a big, warm cosmic hug from God(dess). When I come back from normal church my bum just aches from those hard benches.

If the spiritual structure of your family, culture or society does not serve you as it should, give yourself permission to seek or create one that does. The whole point is to discover your own personal route to your inner and outer God(dess), so it would be silly for me to be prescriptive. However, I do have a couple of suggestions.

Spend time with yourself.

It is amazing how averse we are to being with ourselves! I think it is because we are socialised that alone = lonely = unloved = it proves there is something wrong with me; therefore it is to be avoided at all costs. A lot of people are very fearful of being WITH themselves. I say being *with* themselves as opposed to being *by* themselves because the two are different. We all spend time by ourselves watching TV, reading books, calling friends, Facebooking, BBMing and Tweeting. We are really not with ourselves. We are with the TV, the internet, the book, the cellphone. Our attention is directed outward, to something else. The danger with this is that we miss out on our internal wisdom, on an opportunity to live from the inside out. We do not hear the messages of our body and intuition. Intuition, our most valuable guide, is found in calmness and serenity. It is a soft voice that cannot compete with all the external stimuli with which we assault our senses. To access the wisdom of your body you need to be still and receptive. To access the wisdom of your spirit you need to be still and receptive. To do this you need to spend some time with yourself. Canadian singer-songwriter and poet Tanya Davis wrote a poem entitled "How to be Alone" with a line that says, "resist the urge to hang out with your cellphone". I love that line, because I fully hang out with my cellphone! Learn to be comfortably with yourself, Evelet.

I'm about to use the dreaded m-word. Meditate. Yep, I know it's hard. Your mind, rightly, recognises it as an attempt to erode its control and so it fights you tooth and nail, making meditation difficult. There are various ways to meditate; the trick is to find one that suits you. Beware though, in the beginning they pretty much all feel futile because of the tantrum being throw by your mind, but commit to the process. From what I hear – because I must admit that I fall off the meditation wagon often – with prolonged practice it brings meaning, purpose, stability and perspective to our lives. Even my erratic bouts of meditation leave me feeling more centred, grounded, spiritually connected and less identified with my mind. Just 10 minutes upon waking or before bed is better than nothing. That's what I am currently doing, 10 minutes once or twice a day.

This brings me to another issue: busyness. Don't we just love being busy? I'm convinced that it's our greatest addiction. I enjoy social media, and I always note how many updates are about busyness – grinding, hustling, grafting, missioning. We have made over-extension sexy, yet this chronic busyness is really a sign of malaise. We are scared to just *be*, we think that in order to be worthy we have to be productive. We think we need to earn love by doing, achieving, succeeding, striving. Busyness generally means we are running away from something, and often that something is ourselves. I live in Johannesburg, where exhaustion is a status symbol. You can always squeeze in one more thing. We are busy, busy, busy. Our kids are busy, busy, busy; even our pets have vet and puppy socialisation commitments, and, and, and... We text while we drive. We hoot at any car in front of us that doesn't drive off a split second before the traffic light turns green. We have places to go, things to do, people to meet. Miss B mirrored me very well once when she was about two-and-a-half. We had stopped at a red traffic light on a leisurely Sunday afternoon when she hissed at the car in front of us, "Mooooooooove! Eish, this guy!" Welcome to the rat race; the one who dies standing wins.

I don't think it is a coincidence that there is only one letter's difference between business and busyness. Psychologist Chuck Spezzano[18] says that busyness "attempts to protect us from the fear generated by our shadow figures, the unconscious mind, and our pain. It blocks out soul level gifts, our purpose and our destiny. In our busyness we are trying to run away from feelings of guilt, failure and worthlessness. We drive ourselves onward to prove we are useful and valuable. Yet dark feelings float to the surface in any moment of respite, so we keep pushing on. Our busyness keeps us too busy for love and bonding that would bring about the same success with much less effort." I have a friend who is the master of busyness. He has two jobs, a day job and a night job, with about two free hours in between. These two jobs are not for the money, since he has no dependents. All this hard work leaves him with lots of cash which he uses to buy stuff, like cars, to justify why he needs to work more so he can spend more, so he can work more. Society makes it easy for him to remain a junkie. He is working hard for an honest living, plus he has stuff, and we all want stuff: nice cars, nice clothes and a big fat house which, in his case, is empty – no partner, kids, pets or even plants because he is always working. It doesn't take a genius to recognise that his entire worth is bound up in doing and if he weren't productive he'd be worthless and unworthy. Remember, Evelet, you are not a human *doing* you are a human *being*. You won't cease to exist if you stop doing; in fact it is in being, not doing, that you discover who you truly are. The Buddha described busyness as one of the ways that stops happiness. S L O W down.

Appreciating what you already have fosters happiness and calm. Let what you have be enough, Evie. I am not saying you shouldn't strive for more, but do let what you have be enough. You have probably heard of an attitude of gratitude, an Oprah favourite. Since you can only experience what you are giving your attention to, focusing on the things that you are grateful for instantly upgrades the quality of your present experience. The law of attraction teaches that whatever you give your attention to, you get more of. Thus, an attitude of gratitude has the power to improve your life. Where attention goes energy flows and where energy flows stuff grows.

An attitude of gratitude, I must admit, is not a practice I am enthusiastic about. I couldn't explain my discomfort with the practice until I stumbled on an Abraham-Hicks[19] talk on the practice of appreciation. Often we use contrast to evoke gratitude; for example, I may think "my electricity bill is high, but at least I have electricity; some people don't even have a roof over their heads", or "my husband lazes about all day but at least he is home, unlike many others", "I can't afford that pair of shoes I want, but some people don't even have feet". Okay, maybe that last one is a bit extreme, but my point is that I used contrast between the positive and the negative to evoke a feeling of gratitude for the positive. The problem is that I had to pay some attention to the negative and wherever attention goes energy flows. Thus this common way of evoking gratitude injects a bit of what you don't want into your current and future experience. Appreciation, on the other hand, is entirely in the realm of the positive. When a chocoholic savours a piece of Danish dark chocolate, all focus is on what is right about the experience. This is appreciation! To appreciate Cristiano Ronaldo's washboard stomach it is unnecessary to conjure your husband's beer belly. When you appreciate, all your energy is focused on the positive and it keeps you in the moment. Appreciation is what gratitude wants to be when it grows up. I practice appreciation of the things that fill my heart with joy, such as sunsets, flowers, witty friends, Miss B's near fatal hugs where she snakes her small arms around my neck and chokes me with love, foot massages, cheese... just writing this list makes my soul smile.

Lastly, find something to have faith in. If you have faith, you have hope, and where there is hope there is always a way. When you have a way, you don't have to give up or settle for less than your truest desires; which is the way of the goddess.

Becoming a Goddess: The Care and Feeding of Your Soul

43. Start an appreciation practice. Write a list of the things that you really love. Whenever you experience them be sure to really savour the moment. You don't even have to wait to experience them; just recalling them in an appreciative state of mind is enough. So at least once a week, say on a Sunday, take out your list, go through the items one at a time, and evoke a sense of appreciation for them.

44. Start a meditation practice. There are numerous ways to meditate. You can use a mantra, your breath, or a focal point like a candle flame. You can go for classes on meditations. Some meditations don't even require sitting still, like walking mediations, fishing or gardening. Believe me, there is a meditation practice out there that will suit you. It is an effective way to reduce over-identification with your mind and foster connection with Spirit.

45. Learn to be with you. Occasionally just take a walk by yourself, sit on a park bench or go to a coffee shop alone without any props, no newspapers, books, cellphone, pen, computer, nothing – just you and you.

46. Feed your soul regularly. Honestly evaluate if your traditional spiritual practice is nourishing for your soul, that's if you have one. If it is empty calories for your soul or you haven't got one at all, explore ways to give yourself spiritual sustenance.

47. Honestly examine how you define your worth. Are you worthy because of your roles – manager, wife, mother, helpful friend? Are you worthy because of your possessions? Ask yourself, "What would be left if I lost my roles and possessions?" Somewhere in that answer you will find you. You will need to ask this question often.

48. Divine Intervention: Call on Celtic goddess Nemetona to help you establish your own spiritual practice.

Exalt Your Body

Women are socialised to pretend, settle and call our compromises "life". Our bodies are harder to fool.

~ Harriet Lerner

Do you honour your body, Evie?

It intrigues me how shoddily we treat our bodies, despite knowing that they are an indispensable part of our earthly experience. Tune in to your heartbeat. Can you feel that steady rhythm? When the beating stops, the adventure ends. This should be a very short session, Evie.

You get one body. It is hard to secure spare parts. Take good care of it.

Anyone who has experienced major health problems will tell you how consuming an ailing body is. When you are in serious physical pain it is very hard to experience anything else. We all know this, yet we continue to neglect our bodies. We pull out cigarette after cigarette from boxes clearly warning us about the dangers of smoking. We stuff our bodies with junk food that has less nutritional value than the packaging it comes in. We sit on the couch watching our muscles slowly waste away, as we make jokes like "my body is in shape, round is a shape".

The earth overflows with beauty: starry night skies; sunsets made up of colours that shouldn't go together, like orange and purple, but they do; the sheer poetry in motion that is the fluid, languid, almost arrogant movement of felines and the graceful power of a horse's musculature; majestic waterfalls; flowers and butterflies and even the crazy stripy orange-and-black garb of a bumblebee. I look at such things and bow down to the unrivalled artistry of God(dess). Then I look at people and the soft, placid, "round-shape" baffles me. In the main people are not rewarding to look at. "God(dess) must have created humans on an off day," I conclude. Just then God(dess) directs my gaze to dancers and sports people playing their exquisitely formed bodies like finely tuned instruments and I get it. We, too, are meant to embody a unique beauty, just like all of Mother Goddess's other children. The state of your body will tell you how well you care for it – and cheating with cosmetic surgery doesn't count.

A very intelligent boss of mine had a theory about why we behave as if we are immortal: because we humans are conscious of our consciousness, we are burdened with the awareness that we can die. This knowledge, she postulated, could easily paralyse you. You can be scared into immobility by the idea that, while crossing the road, you can be hit by a car and die; while walking down the stairs you can slip, fall, break your neck and die; while having breakfast you can choke on a rice crispy and Snap, Crackle, Pop you are dead. Death is lurking, everywhere – cue spooky music. For us to be able to function despite this, we have to believe that it won't happen to us. This way, we can go about the business of living. People understand that death happens – to other people – but never quite believe that it will happen to them. You know someone who died of lung cancer, but you continue to smoke; you know someone who died of a stroke, but you have your own lane at the McDonald's drive-by; you know someone who died in a horrific car accident, yet you send text messages while you drive. Why? Because you are immortal, of course. There is a billboard I used to drive past, advertising life insurance. It screamed, in big bold letters "IF YOU DIE WE WILL GIVE MONEY TO YOUR FAMILY". *If*, not when. Seemingly dying is uncertain. Trust not your mind, dear one, for it doth fornicate with thee. You are not immortal. Keep that shit up and your body will degenerate much quicker than necessary. Hang on while I get off my soapbox. I don't expect that little outburst of mine to change your relationship with your body much, so I am going to give you other reasons why you should show your body more care and respect:

1. Your body is a well of wisdom.
2. How you treat your body affects your mood.
3. Your body is your gateway to all the pleasures earthly life has to offer.

Have you ever noticed the relationship that young children have with their bodies? They celebrate their bodies, they enjoy them, they revel in them, but most importantly they respect and heed them. Children respect the wisdom of their bodies, perhaps because they have little else to go on. They eat when they are hungry. They sleep when they are tired. They fart and burp when they are gassy. They go when they gotta go. If the person picking them up feels creepy, they cry. You and I, on the other hand, will get into a lift or walk down an alley with a creepy stranger while every fibre in our bodies is screaming that this person is not to be trusted. But turning on our heels and running would be silly and impolite, so we go against the wisdom of our bodies. Miss B refused to take sweets from a nice man while we waited in an airport lounge. Not only did she turn down the sweets, she refused to make eye contact with him. I recounted this to a friend, who then shared a chilling story: Remember the disappearance of Madeleine McCann, the British girl who disappeared while holidaying with her parents in Portugal? Apparently Madeleine's mother recalled how the previous day a guy who looked like the man seen luring her child away had been trying to talk to Madeleine. The child gave the man a cold reception, similar to what Miss B did to the airport lounge guy. The mother had then said to Madeleine, "C'mon, baby, say 'hi' to the nice man". Madeleine had known that this man was bad news until her mom had indicated otherwise. That story gave me chills. Small children know innately what most adults have forgotten: our bodies are wise. I, too, often get a visceral response to people who have negative intentions, I feel cold and my skin crawls when meeting them for the first time. Through hard-earned experience I have learned to be wary of people who elicit this initial response in me. My body knows.

Your body knows how to keep life coursing through you. It knows what you need. Take cravings, for instance. You know, people occasionally have cravings to ingest non-food items like pencils and chalk. This usually happens when the body has a mineral deficiency of some sort. You then crave whatever item contains the mineral your body needs. You don't have to know what mineral you are deficient in or where to get it because your body knows!

Your body reveals your mind, heart and soul. Your body, through physical illness, signals your mental and emotional imbalances. Physical problems begin as dis-ease in the mental, emotional and spiritual bodies long, sometimes years, before manifestation of the physical symptoms. The nature of the mind is reflected in the state of the body. Even identical twins are most alike at birth because, as they develop their unique personalities, their bodies change to reflect their state of mind. For example, a hunched over, closed posture indicates issues of sorrow, fear and anxiety. The body is literally closed up and weighed down. You can work backwards from a body issue to decipher the mind issue. The issues are in your tissues. For example, according to Debbie Shapiro, author of *Your Body Speaks Your Mind,* a heart attack results from a heart that is overwhelmed by a build-up of unexpressed hurt, loss, grief or resistance to love. This doesn't sound surprising, considering that men, who tend to suppress their emotions more often than women, are the most susceptible to heart attacks as they age – as if at some point the heart can't take it any more and it attacks them. We get constipated when we have issues with surrendering or letting go; the body mirrors the mind by literally holding on to shit it should let go of. We get a sore throat when there is an area of our life where we are restricting our self-expression. Blood pressure becomes too high when we have anger, frustration and resistance to doing something that we are not really into, such as a job we really don't care for beyond the pay cheque. Your thumbs represent worry and anxiety. The left side of your body represents feminine issues and the right, masculine issues such as leading and providing. Soon after leaving my job to become "funemployed" I broke my right thumb. I had doubts I was not acknowledging about my ability to provide for myself without a stable income and this is how my body communicated this repressed anxiety to me.

I recall once having such an emotionally tumultuous week that I told my boss to "shove it". He sent me an inquiry about something I felt was a waste of my time, so I responded by explicitly describing what I recommend he should do with his request. Had I been a cartoon character I would have had a dark, thunderous cloud above my head. My emotional range was limited to two: angry and weepy. Everything in my life was, had been, and was going to be, bleak. I declared to a friend that I was depressed. When she inquired about the cause, I answered honestly, "I don't know, I just am." Fortunately, I identified the source of my dark mood soon after. Miss B had suffered from flu for two weeks. Every night I would be awoken by an hour-long coughing fit at around 3 am, so I hadn't had a single night of uninterrupted sleep for two weeks. I had also had a bit of a cold I couldn't shake, so I had suspended my exercise regime. In fact the whole household was sick and, because we had no appetite and couldn't taste our food, I'd been lax about preparing decent meals. This was the recipe for my meltdown: junk food, inadequate rest and lack of exercise. Many people are unaware of or disregard the impact their physical condition has on their moods. We don't care for our bodies as we should and are willing to pay the price, which we consider to be a muffin-top oozing over our jeans, a lacklustre complexion and a lack of energy, but we seldom realise that we also pay with our emotional state.

There are four main neurochemicals that affect mood: serotonin, dopamine, epinephrine and endorphin. They are affected by, among other things, how much we exercise, what we eat and how well we rest. Exercise has a positive effect on all four of these neurochemicals, resulting in enhanced mood, and reduced anxiety, stress and depression. Food also acts on brain chemistry. We all know that we can go from frown to crown on a good bar of dark chocolate. This is because chocolate – the darker the better – stimulates the release of serotonin; so do complex carbohydrates. Various foods impact the different neurochemicals. For instance Omega 3s are good for endorphin levels and protein stimulates the production of dopamine and epinephrine. On the other hand, sugary, fatty carbohydrates found in junk food are more likely to repay you with memory loss and depression. Most junk food contains aspartame and MSG, excitotoxins that have been linked to depression. Finally, lack of sleep depletes the mood-regulating neurotransmitters; as a result, sleep deprivation will make you short-tempered and susceptible to depression.

Perhaps, as we like to convince ourselves, the physical consequences of our lifestyle may be subject to some cosmic lottery. We all have anecdotal evidence, "Uncle Rush had a 40-a-day habit and lived to be a 100 and Mary, the health nut, was run over by a taxi while jogging." However, I guarantee you that your diet, rest and exercise habits are impacting your mood right now.

The Goddess Academy gives a course called "Joy and the Art of Divine Living", which is about lasting joy. One of the mainstays we learn about living joyfully is learning to stay present, in this moment. Evelet, if you are waiting for some future condition in order to be joyful you are going to be waiting for a long time, because the future never comes. All of life's WOWness is in the present moment. Only in the present do you get your presents. All your power lies in the present moment. Everything you can affect is in the now moment. All experiences (including bliss) can only be had in the now moment, not in the past or the future. The past and the future are mental constructs. The NOW moment is the only point in time within which you can experience life. Your body is your ticket to enjoying life's bounty. Minds are no good at being in the present moment, but bodies can only be here, in the now. If you learn how to stay out of your mind and in your body you will be available to receive the gifts of life. Imagine tasting your beloved through a kiss, witnessing in his eyes the love he feels for you, feeling that love in how he wraps you in his arms, laying your head on his chest to listen to his heartbeat and getting lost in his musky scent. Utter WOWness, Evie. No mind here, just your body, heart and soul.

Exalt your body, dear one. Understand that it is more than a thing on which you hang your designer clothes. Show it lots of love and appreciation. I was born into a family of women at war with their bodies. My early memories include the distinct aroma of Black Forest Herbal Tea perpetually brewing on our stove. My mother and my aunt seemed to live on the stuff. My other aunt appeared to subsist on a fizzy cooldrink and appetite suppressant combo, while my mother favoured fad diets and visits to The French Clinic. Hence I gained a distinct impression that bodies were wayward and had to be constantly monitored and starved into submission. I haven't been anything close to chubby since shedding my baby fat in early adolescence, but I am absolutely terrified of being fat. I am hyper-aware of what I put into my body and the effect that it has on my figure. If I am feeling heavy I start wearing my "fat" clothes and avoid looking in the mirror. I am also aware how unhealthy all this is and, since having a girl-child, I've become sensitive about not passing on this pathology to her. I consciously remind myself that my body's job is not to look good in clothes. I remind myself that, yes, I should pay attention to what I eat, but so I can be healthy and feel good. Looking good should be a side benefit of a good diet and exercise regime, not the goal. Having had an easy pregnancy, complication-free birth and a healthy baby helped me see my body as more than a clothes hanger. My body successfully incubated life with no help from me; for six months it provided exclusive nourishment for my baby and, through its senses, continues to experience the many blessings of motherhood. Such recognitions help me promote my body from a collection of measurements to a reliable servant, guide and gift. It's an ongoing process for me, treating my body with awe, care and respect. I recognise that it is my passport to the land of WOWness.

Becoming a Goddess: Honouring Your Body

49. Do an honest audit of how well you care for your body:
    a. Diet
    b. Exercise
    c. Rest
    d. Bad and stupid habits – smoking, texting while driving, drinking too much coffee and alcohol and not enough water, etc.

50. Own and consult a book on the mind-body connection, such as Debbie Shapiro's *Your Body Speaks Your Mind* or Louise Hay's *Love Yourself, Heal Your Life*. Start using your body to recognise – so you can heal – your mental, emotional and spiritual dis-eases.

51. Write a list of all the things you need to be, do and have before you will give yourself permission to enjoy life more. For example, maybe you'll go out more when you have a boyfriend, or you'll start wearing nice clothes after you lose weight, or you'll cook nice meals when you are no longer cooking for one.
    a. Ask yourself why you need these conditions to be fulfilled first. Why can't you be worthy right now? What is stopping you from being enough right now?
    b. Imagine that these conditions will never be fulfilled. What if you never, ever have another boyfriend? It could happen, you know. What if you just never get to lose the weight? Are you going to keep your joy hostage in the future

forever, or are you going to start living as if you were born worthy of WOWness?

52. Practice being present. Whenever you catch yourself unnecessarily stuck in your head, occupy your body instead. Here are two quick exercise to help you get out of your mind and into your body:

a. Deliberately heighten your senses. Focus on each of your senses, one at a time for at least a minute each. Ask yourself, "What do I see?" For at least a minute really look at your surroundings – notice colours, textures, things that are nearby and things that are far away. Then move on to another sense. What do I feel against my skin? Pay attention to how your clothes feel against your skin. The pressure of the chair you are sitting in. The temperature, is there a breeze? Can you feel the air conditioning? Do this for at least a minute then move on to another sense. What do I smell? What do I hear? What flavours can I identify in my mouth?

b. Contract your vaginal muscles. Squeeze them and hold the contraction as long as you can. It will bring your awareness into your body, it feels good and you'll look like you know a cool secret.

53. Pay homage to your body. Your body has served you well, more often than not, despite your neglect and lack of appreciation.

a. List all the ways that your body has and continues to serve you; then thank it in whichever way feels right. You could write it a poem, love letter or song and, if you feel moved to, post it on The Goddess Academy Facebook group.

b. If you have body-image issues, pick a day you will use weekly to just love and nurture your body. Pamper it with luxurious products, maybe a massage or a long bubble bath; then stand in front of the mirror, caressing it with love and acceptance. Express your acceptance out loud for all those body parts that you reject: your "too big" thighs, "flabby" arms, "saggy" breasts, hold them and tell them out loud that you love and accept them as they are. If that feels untrue, then tell them that you want to love and accept them as they are. If that still feels inauthentic, try "I am willing to be willing to love and accept you as you are".

Every day, stand in front of the mirror and, out loud, say one thing you like about your body.

54. Practice some food sex. This is a conscious, sensual way to eat food as meditation. When you have some time to yourself, get your favourite food, put it on a nice plate using your fingers instead of cutlery. Pretend that you are an alien seeing this food for the very first time. Take a moment just to look at it. Notice all its colours and textures. Then smell it. Imagine the smell infusing all your cells. Next, take a piece, with your hand if possible, feel the texture first on your fingers, then on your lips, caress your lips with the food first before putting it in your mouth, then lick your lips. Pay attention to those initial flavours on the tip of your tongue. Finally, take your first bite, close your eyes and savour. Repeat as you please.

55. Divine Inspiration: All the goddesses of sexuality love, appreciate and celebrate their bodies. Look to the likes of Aphrodite and Freyja to help you exalt yours.

Change Your Mind

It is never too late – in fiction or in life – to revise.

~ Nancy Thayer

Who is the boss of you, Evie?

Miss B is constantly trying to see how much she can get away with, so we are engaged in a perpetual battle of wills. During one of our power struggles, I had an ace up my sleeve. Her fourth birthday was coming up and she was really looking forward to it. I picked up the phone and pretended to cancel the birthday party. She quickly conceded to my demands. She was quiet and docile after that. In the car, on the way to school, she finally said, "Mommy, you are the boss of me."

Who is the boss of you, Evie?

Who gets to decide who, what and how you are? What if I told you that there is no higher authority in your life? There may be a higher authority in your life, but you have to give him/her/they/it permission to be your boss, meaning that technically you are still the boss. You are the writer, producer, director, and co-creator of your life. You are in charge of the script being played out by you and the people you have cast as family, friends, villains, lovers, colleagues, even "random" once-off encounters.

Throughout your life, your mind tells stories to speak of its journey. We are constantly telling stories to ourselves and others. We tell a story with our lives, the story of our beliefs. Everything that is part of this story starts with a belief. Beliefs are fixed, conscious or unconscious, thoughts that we have made our truths.

There is absolutely nothing stopping you from having what you want, except your beliefs on the subject, whatever they may be. As you think, so it is. It cannot be any other way. This is the nature of the universe. Your thoughts are creative. You are a goddess, a creator. Creativity is at the very core of you. As a creator you have complete free will to produce whatever you wish. This you do through the process of attraction.

We like to think that life happens to us, when we choose victimhood over goddesshood. As doormats we choose to believe in luck, fate and coincidences. But it ain't so Evie, we get what we believe.

Think about how many repeats of your own life you've gone through – different faces, characters and sets, all with the same damn plot. Let's see if I remember how the story goes: You have worked in eight different companies and each time you have ended up with an insecure, manipulative boss who sabotages your career advancement. Or are you the one with the psycho ex? You found a nice mentally stable mate to help you recover from your trauma by psycho ex, but for some inexplicable reason, the replacement is also starting to exhibit psycho tendencies. In fact, all your partners eventually morph into the same character. Coincidence? The universe says not. You are using the Law of Attraction all the time. All experiences, things and people in your life (including goddess bootcamp) are there because you have drawn them into your energy field. There are no exceptions to this rule, no chance meetings, no coincidences, no accidents, no divine intervention, no external forces stopping you from having what you want, and no one rewarding you either. Our beliefs may be conscious or unconscious, but they are creative nonetheless. Nothing can happen in your life without you believing it can.

Through that which you create you get to know yourself. As you create, you discover more of who you are, from observing your creation – your life, your world. It's like your mind is a projector and your life is the projected image, generated by the beliefs you hold about yourself, life and everything. So by observing your life you can decide what is not working for you, and you can change it by changing your beliefs. If you don't like what you are seeing on the movie screen of your life, Evelet, change your mind. As women, we have a reputation for being capricious, changing our minds and moods like the weather. Relative to men, we are pretty mutable. This is not a bad thing, Evie. Harness this ability to change your mind about important things, like your story. What kind of story are you telling at the moment? Is it fit for a goddess? Are you telling a happy story or a sad story? Is it a triumphant story of healing or a tragedy? Have you cast yourself as the queen, a little vulnerable princess, or the bitter, ugly stepsister? Are you the party-starter or the martyr? A goddess or a doormat? Does your story add to or take away from the quality of your life and the realisation of your desires? You are the writer, director, producer and casting agent, so you get to choose. If you are not feeling this story, change your mind, Evie.

We carry around all these limiting beliefs that sabotage our dreams and desires. Do you recognise any of these, Evelet?

• I'm not good/thin/smart/attractive enough. • I don't have enough money. • I need to make others happy so I won't be rejected. • I can't be happy until he/she changes. • I have to earn other people's approval to feel good about myself. • If I let people really get to know me, they won't like me. • I have to stay in this relationship/job/city/country because this is the best I can do. • I can't be happy until this relationship/career/body is different. • If he/she really loved me, then he/she would... • I need to do more and more to be worthy. • I don't know what I want. • I shouldn't put my needs before the needs of others. • All good things come to an end. • I'm responsible for other people's happiness and they're responsible for mine. • I don't deserve love, success, money, fame... • If I pursue my own interests, my relationships will suffer. • I don't have time to nurture myself. • It's too late for me to change. • If I speak my mind, I'll be rejected. • By now I should be a lot more successful than I am. • I'd better not be too happy, or I'll attract misfortune. • Things will never work out for me. • I shouldn't have to ask my partner for what I want. • I'm a bad/unlovable person. • I need fear to motivate me and keep me in check. • I'll never make enough money. • I'll always have to struggle, while others have it easier. • I can't do it.

Change your mind, Evelet. That is all you need to do, but do bear in mind that the physical does not change as quickly as the energetic. When you change the belief that created your overeating, couch-potato lifestyle, this change in belief will cause a change in your behaviour. You will start making different lifestyle choices, but it will take weeks, maybe even months, for you to shed the extra weight, drop the cholesterol and build some respectable muscle- and lung capacity. You may change the belief that leads you to attract controlling, jealous psycho lovers, and this change in belief may lead you to quickly dump the current psycho. But if you are married to or have lovelets with the psycho, it may be more challenging to untangle yourself from the experience and manifest a new one that is reflective of your changed mind. In cases where you "cannot" change your reality, there is something else you can change. Change your perspective.

Perspective is everything. You can choose to see yourself as a victim of circumstances or you can choose to reframe the negative and learn from your creations. Many situations are similar to a chrysalis, which seems like the end to the caterpillar but, to the butterfly, it is the beginning. A goddess understands that very few things are absolute. Always seek an empowering perspective, Evie.

How many times have you been stuck in a traffic jam having a full meltdown, only to discover that it clears up really quickly just over the rise? A minor delay, unworthy of getting your knickers in a knot – except of course you couldn't see over the rise, so for all you knew it could have been a massive roadblock where they are detaining people like you for unpaid traffic fines. We experience many situations like these in life where, if we'd had an elevated view, we would have seen the situation better and realised that it was actually not such a big deal. Change your perspective where you can. When you can't see things from a different angle, you can still draw strength from choosing to believe it only looks bad because you don't have a better view. Reaching for a higher perspective can be extremely empowering and freeing.

There was a time when my relationship with Spirit had broken down, over a boy. I'd recently asked Spirit for a soul mate, in response to a longing I could only describe as a desire for "big love". I naively concluded that it must be the kind of love you get from a soul mate and not a pedestrian Mr Right, so I prayed for a soul mate. Soon I was in the throes of the most intense love affair of my life. I thought I had found The One. Just as I was basking in my good fortune, the romance rapidly deteriorated into my worst nightmare. My angel morphed into a demon. He behaved in ways that uncannily evoked all the fears and insecurities I worked so hard to suppress, instead of doing what I'd hoped he would, which was to love them away. I was hurt, confused and felt betrayed by God(dess). Maybe the real God(dess) was not the loving God(dess) I had been frolicking with in parks and gardens, but that Sunday school God who favoured hellfire and brimstone, I thought. I wanted nothing to do with that insecure and vengeful God. I was preparing to break up with him – God, not the guy. I was not ready to give up on the guy just yet, when I came across this tale:

One day in heaven, a little soul asked God what she was made of. God replied, "You, like everyone else, are made of Love." The little soul then enquired about the nature of Love. God informed her that Love is all there is. Sensing the little soul's dissatisfaction with this response, God reassured her, "You are not the first soul to be curious about your nature, for it is one thing knowing who you are and something richer and deeper experiencing who you are. Hence I created the world, a place where you can discover who you are, through being it. I send souls there as human beings."

The little soul pleaded to be sent to the world, so she could experience who she was. "Which aspect of Love would you like to be?" enquired God. "Love manifests in many forms such as compassion, forgiveness, courage and generosity."

Impulsively the little soul picked forgiveness – it sounded grand! God pointed out that to experience forgiveness she needed someone to forgive. The little Soul had absolutely no one to forgive. "Whom will I forgive?" she wondered aloud. Another soul, who had been listening to this exchange, volunteered to give her an opportunity to forgive him.

"You would choose to leave Heaven and all its joys to go down to the world with me?" she exclaimed, "Why?"

"Because I am your kin and I love you," said the generous soul, sincerely. To which the Little Soul beamed gratefully, "How can I ever thank you?"

The more experienced soul replied warily, "When I hurt you, cause you emotional or physical pain and I give you an opportunity to be forgiving, right at that moment please remember who I am."

The Little Soul said, somewhat offended, "Oh! I will never forget you. You are my kind and loving brother."

Then off they went to the world together, future victim and perpetrator, to experience forgiveness."

I understood from this parable that every experience has multiple perspectives. I also realised that Spirit always answers my prayers, usually far more efficiently than I could've imagined. Spirit sees the bigger picture in my requests and responds to the higher, not the base, yearning. When I ask for a fish to satiate my immediate hunger, Spirit teaches me how to call Mr Delivery. My longing for "big love" was actually an inner craving for self-love, and Spirit sent me an experience I could only conquer by valuing the love of self, over the love of another. I was literally in a situation where I could not love myself and remain in the relationship. Choosing myself was how I got to experience "big love". Now in situations where I am inclined towards victimhood, I seek a different, higher perspective.

Becoming a Goddess: Writing a New Story

56. Examine your life story. If your life were a movie or a book, what would its name be? What kind of story would it be – a happy story, a love story, a sad story, a tragedy, a story of struggle and suffering, a story of martyrdom, an exciting story, a boring story, or a triumphant story of rising above great odds?
    a. Are you happy with the story that you have written so far? Could it use some revision, or perhaps what you truly want is a whole new story?
    b. Identify what kind of story you want to tell with your life. Describe the story in your journal. Give it a name and a genre. Start telling the new story to your self (through your inner chatter) and to others.

57. Change what you create.
    a. Look at your current life and identify the limiting beliefs that you would like to change. A belief is called limiting when it opposes what you would like to create. For example, if you want to create wealth but you believe that money is the root of all evil, that's a limiting belief. You can identify your limiting beliefs by:
       i. Paying attention to your internal chatter and to the things you say to other people, e.g., "men are dogs", "all good things come to an end", "I should be so lucky".
       ii. Using affirmations. State what you want as if you already have it and listen to the backchat from your inner voices. If your inner voices disagree with the affirmation, they

will tell you why they disagree and that will be the limiting belief you hold regarding whatever you are affirming. Examples of affirmations:

1. I am worthy of the life of my dreams.
2. Success comes easily to me.
3. I accept myself as I am.

b. Identify how you feel about achieving your desired reality. If you have limiting beliefs, you will either feel hopeless, helpless or worthless. Hopelessness – My desire cannot be fulfilled, it's impossible. If you are feeling hopeless ask yourself, "Why is this goal unattainable?" Helplessness – My desire can be fulfilled but I lack the ability to fulfil it. It's impossible for me. If you are feeling helpless as yourself, ask, "What skills do I lack to attain this goal?" Worthlessness – I don't deserve to fulfil this goal, because of something I am (not) or have (not) done. If you are feeling worthless, ask yourself, "Why don't I deserve to achieve this goal?" Uncovering beliefs is all about asking questions. Once you have identified the limiting belief, ask more questions. Beliefs tend to come in clusters. Continue to probe your beliefs until you feel you have uncovered all the limiting beliefs that stand in the way of your new story.

c. Identify the benefits of your current reality. Any belief, however limiting, benefits you in some way otherwise you would not have it. To successfully change a limiting belief it is important to identify its benefits to you. You can use the Pros and Cons Square. Say your goal is to get back to the weight you were 10 years ago, this is what your square may look like:

I want to lose weight so I can be the same size I was 10 years ago	
PROS	CONS
- I will be healthier - I will be more confident - I will look good - I will be able to run around with my kids - I will be able to get back into those old clothes I still love	- I will have to buy new clothes - My best friend is going to be jealous - I will probably attract the unwanted attention of my pervert boss - I will have to commit to maintaining the weight loss and I'm not sure I can keep it up - I will become one of them, the calorie-counting gym bunnies that I've been judging
I want to remain the size I am right now	
PROS	CONS
- I won't have to change a thing - If I don't try I can't fail - Women are nicer to me because I am not physically threatening - My husband doesn't act jealous the way he used to when I was thin - I don't have to deal with unwanted male attention	- I am unhealthy - I get tired very quickly - I can't play with my kids - I feel unattractive - My confidence has taken a knock

Push yourself to have at least seven points under each. It's only when you start pushing yourself that you get your underlying motives.

I know a lady who struggled to lose weight because feeling fat made her feel safe. She had steadily gained weight after she had been raped seven years before. Until she uncovered the fact that a big benefit of being fat was that it made her believe she was unattractive to men – and therefore safe from sexual violation – she could not have shaken the weight off. Only after seeking other ways to help her feel safe (she took self-defence classes) was she able to shake off the weight.

Other tools for freeing you from limiting beliefs are:
- Emotional Freedom Technique (EFT).
- Hypnosis.
- Prayer. If you believe in a higher power that can intervene, ask for help to free yourself from the limiting belief. "I no longer choose to believe this, what I want now is... Help me achieve this with grace, in perfect, harmonious and miraculous ways."

58. Divine intervention: The Hopi kachina (spirit) Butterfly Maiden and the Hawaiian Pele are the goddesses to call on when you need help emerging from any situation in which you feel stuck.

Say "Yes!" to Life

Life happens at the rate of acceptance.

~ Humblebree

Are you a "yes ma'am", Evie?

Any goddess worth her salt knows the importance of saying "No", but do you know when to say "Yes!" Evelet?

We become trapped in time when we say "no" to certain experiences. We literally get frozen in a point in time, when we refuse to accept something. Energy healers and shamans will tell you about soul fragments – personas or inner children to psychologists. These soul fragments are parts of you that have remained stuck – usually as a result of an overwhelming incident or event, which is usually, but not necessarily, negative.

Imagine that you are taking a walk in nature somewhere with your family. Your mother is walking ahead of you all. She gets to a suspension bridge, which you must all walk across in order to cross the raging river below. When she is in the middle of the bridge, it snaps and she falls into the rapids beneath. You witness all this. Chances are you will experience the whole thing as if it is in slow motion and your immediate thought will be how to stop it. If there is nothing you can do physically, you will settle for an energetic and resounding "No!" to what is happening. It is in such moments, and others that may be less dramatic, that we leave a part of us behind. A part of us remains stuck in that moment where we said "no", where we refused to accept life as it unfolded. You may from then on become terrified of bridges, whether they are over water or over land. You may fear bodies of water, even inert ones like swimming pools or koi ponds. You may develop an aversion to family outings.

When you go for therapy, an energy healer may say you need to retrieve a fragment of your soul that got stuck in that moment in time, a psychotherapist may say you need to integrate that part of you that got stuck in that experience. This is necessary to make you whole.

Imagine that all of the events that have occurred in your life are like short films playing in a cinema. You can come in and out of any cinema as you please and watch the film playing out on the screen, through memories. However, the cinemas screening events that you refused to accept are locked and a piece of you is trapped inside, having to relive that moment over and over again. As soon as you accept what has happened the door will open magically and you will be free to go. The more you say "no" to life the more you trap yourself and dissipate your energy. You become mentally, emotionally and energetically fragmented. There is literally less and less of you to go around. Which makes it harder for you to do anything. The less of you there is the harder life becomes.

One of the Spiritual Laws covered in Deepak Chopra's book *The Seven Spiritual Laws of Success*[20] is the Law of Least Effort. This law teaches that it is in the nature of all beings to accomplish with ease and effortlessness. It is easy and effortless for your body to keep your heart pumping, blood circulating and hair growing. A flower blossoms effortlessly. The sun shines with ease. There is no "grinding", "missioning" or "hustling" when a fish swims or a star twinkles. This is how life is meant to be. This is how life is, when we come from love. Remember, Daughter of Eve, the opposite of love is not hate. It is fear. When we come from a fearful place, a "No!" place, things become a struggle. One of the things you can do to put the Law of Least Effort into action is to accept things and people exactly as they are in this moment, not as you wish they were. Reflect on how much more fun anything is when you don't have any expectation or need for it to be other than it is. Chopra points out, "When you struggle against this moment, you struggle against the entire universe. You can intend for things to be different in the future, but in this moment, accept things as they are." Struggling against the entire universe. Imagine how much energy that takes, Evie. Just the thought is exhausting.

When I got my first tattoo, my most pressing concern, predictably, was the pain. The tattoo artist assured me that it was unlikely to be as painful as I imagined, but he implored me to remember to breathe – to avoid fainting. Apparently some people, in response to the real or anticipated pain, hold their breath to the point of passing out! Crazy, isn't it? Holding your breath until you pass out. Our breath is our primal "YES" or "NO" to life and its accompanying experiences. Our very first act as independent beings is an inhale, and our last an exhale. We hold our breath to resist, when we fear pain, feel stress and even when we climb on the bathroom scale after a weekend of the awesome twosome – carbs and alcohol. Conversely, when we say yes to an experience we tend to literally take it in with a deep breath. We deeply inhale the first morning of a long-awaited holiday, we infuse our being with relaxation as we sink in to a warm bath after a long day, we receive the embrace of a loved one with a deep heart-warming breath.

According to author Margot Anand,[21] the average person inhales about half a litre of air per breath, when in fact our lungs can accommodate seven times that much when fully expanded. Babies are great breathers. They have little resistance to life. They breathe deep into their bellies, which inflate as they fully take in

101

the oxygen and deflate as they exhale all the CO_2. Adults breathe much more shallowly. Instead of breathing into our bellies, many of us breathe into the top of our lungs – known as "the inhibited breathing pattern", from which many people suffer.

Place your hands on your upper chest and take a deep breath, deep enough to push your hands out. Exhale fully. Take two more breaths of this nature. Now place your hands on your abdomen and breathe deeply into your abdomen. Fill your belly with enough air to push your hands out. Exhale fully from the belly, via the lungs and through the nostrils. Feel yourself expel all the CO_2. Do this twice more. Can you feel the difference? A deep breath is superior to a shallow breath and a belly breath is more energising and grounding than one that stops at the lungs.

Shallow breathing is like driving with your foot on the brake. Incidentally, the inhibited breathing pattern is most prevalent in women. For whatever reason, women generally take in less life than men. Are you one of these women, Evie? Ask yourself what about life you disapprove of. What are you resisting? What are you afraid of? What is so stressful that you have to say "no" to it continuously by limiting the amount of life you take in? When you deprive yourself of oxygen, you lose out on its numerous benefits. Among other things, oxygen:

- Is an immune builder
- Gives you energy
- Promotes healing
- Counteracts ageing
- Calms the mind
- Stabilises the nervous system

You need to trust life in order to go into it with open arms, which may explain to some extent why women are the shallowest breathers. We generally feel more unsafe in the world than men. One of the ways to trust life is by realising that nothing on this physical earth can really do you any harm. If you see yourself as being more than a body, that is. Your body can and will get hurt, and eventually expire. Your heart can and will be broken. But if you allow it, it will heal. Your mind can be lost and recovered. So, yes, your body, mind and heart are pretty fragile, but your spirit endures. If you see yourself as a spiritual being with a body, as opposed to a physical being with a soul, you can get to a point where you understand that nothing in this earthly realm can do you any real harm. I remember the first time I read Neale Donald Walsch's book *Conversations with God* I was offended when I read that God doesn't care what happens to me. It said that God isn't too fussed by what is happening to me here on earth because he knows that no real harm can befall me. It is like when your child is playing in his room, he may fall off the bed and break an arm, but you are generally not all that concerned with what he is up to because you know that no real harm can befall him in his bedroom. Similarly, no real, incurable harm can befall your spirit during your incarnation. This is a hard one to get your head around, so don't bother. Rather take it into your meditations. Let Spirit help you get this one. Let your spirit help you trust life. When you trust life you can jump into it and let the flow take you where it may – and usually it leads to fabulously juicy WOWness.

Be generous with your breath, and stingy with something else: your attention. Breathe. You should be extremely careful about what you pay attention to. Few things will improve the quality of your life quicker than being selective about what you pay attention to. Attention is a very powerful thing. Along with the breath it is a primordial YES! Attention is to everything what steroids are to that guy who looks like he swallowed a gym.

Attention is how you say "yes" to things. You cannot experience something that you are not paying any attention to. How many times have you discovered a mysterious cut on your body and it only starts aching once you notice it? Granted, sometimes things grab your attention without your permission, like if a car were to ram into you. On the other hand, you can spend an entire movie sending SMSes and miss it completely because, despite being in the cinema, your attention was elsewhere.

Energy is the building block of everything. So it stands to reason that to increase something, anything, you need to invest more energy into it. Remember, your thoughts are energetic, so where attention goes energy flows and where energy flows stuff grows. Too often we pay attention to things that we definitely do not want more of. For example, we love to fight against things we do not want – the war against drugs, crime, AIDS, global warming, etc. – and fighting demands a lot of energy. The last time I checked, globally and locally, we had a bigger drug problem than ever before, crime in SA is continually on the increase, and our HIV infection rates are still frightening.

To many living creatures, attention is love. People, pets and plants thrive when given attention. Charismatic people are often described with phrases such as, "He makes you feel like the only person in the room". Attention makes us feel valued. Often, any form of attention is better than no attention at all. A neglected puppy may chew on your shoes just to get your attention, even if it comes as a spank on the nose. A neglected teenager may turn into the school slut, because any attention is better than no attention at all. Think of the black sheep of your family, apparently every family has one. They sure get a lot of attention for their antics! Do you think that person would get as much attention if they were not bad, rebellious or difficult? Do you think they would continue their behaviour if people stopped giving them so much attention? Attention is love. Treat it that way. Only give it to things you want more of. If you don't like something, stop thinking about it, stop talking about it, stop giving it energy. We often do the opposite. We give most of our attention to things we don't want. We tell people how tired we feel, how broke we are, how much we hate our jobs. A classic one is the amount of attention we give to lousy men; abusers, jerks, liars and cheaters. We can talk about them for hours, and we do! How much of our energy is sent in the direction of good men – the ones who protect us, encourage us and generally make us feel good? Not nearly as much as we devote to jerks! Breaking up with them and talking about it, making up with them and talking about it, calling them jerks, supporting friends who are either making up or breaking up with them, trying to understand them, trying to redeem them, and on and on and on. This is how I'd like you to view attention from now on Evie: you give it attention you say to it, "Yes, I invite you into my experience." You give it attention you say, "Supersize it for me, please." You give it attention you say, "I love this, give me more".

It takes a lot of discipline to keep pulling your attention back from things that you don't want and giving it to things you'd like more of. If it were easy we'd all have great lives. The path to WOWness is simple, but it ain't easy. Do it anyway; you deserve it.

Becoming a Goddess: Getting More of the Right Things

59. Free yourself with a "Yes". Look at the places where you are stuck due to refusal to accept and find a way to free yourself. You can do it with a psychologist, with an energy therapist, a shaman, a hypnotist or by yourself using EFT. Holotropic Breathwork worked really well for me. You judge whether it is something you can do by yourself or if you require external support. You know where you are stuck. Phobias are a good indication of being stuck. So are patterns from the past that keep repeating themselves. Places of stuckness are pretty obvious – that event or person from the past that you regularly revisit and revise in your mind. Free yourself by accepting what has been and move on.

60. Breathe.
    a. Whenever you remember your breathing, deepen it. Breathe from the belly, like an infant.
    b. Whenever you find yourself resisting a situation, force yourself to accept it with your breath by breathing deeply through it.
    c. Take up an activity that makes you breathe hard, such as exercise, yoga, big belly laughs – try laughing yoga – or whatever else encourages your primal YES to life. Just Breathe.

61. Learn to recognise that the opposite of Love really is Fear. Whenever you feel yourself withholding love – refusing to accept, judging or rejecting a person or situation – ask yourself, "What am I afraid of?"

62. Cultivate Trust
    a. Develop a relationship with the spirit within you. In your meditation (you've started to meditate, right?) intend to discover the self that is not your mind, body or emotions. Once you have a solid relationship with your own spirit you get a better perspective of who you are and what really matters in life.
    b. Develop a relationship with Spirit outside of you. If you can develop a trusting relationship with Spirit (God, Source, Creator, the Universe) you don't have to be in charge of everything and you can know that Spirit has got your back. Even when things look rough you can trust that it will all have a happy ending. When you trust in a happy ending you can say "Yes" to whatever is happening in the moment.
    c. Have a Yes day. Pick a day on which you will ask God(dess) to look out for you, fully and completely. On that day, explicitly give God(dess) permission to be the boss of your life. Then accept all invites you receive that day, be they via email, text, phone or person. Accept them all and see how the day turns out. Then consider upgrading to a Yes week, then a Yes month. February is my Yes month. Who knows, soon enough you may just decide to have a Yes year or even a Yes life! Generally the things that are most mind-blowing in life are not arrived at by what our little minds can conceive. It is when we go with the flow that we end up in amazing places and spaces.

63. Divine Intervention: Saying "Yes!" to life requires courage, and Hindu goddess Kali is a great one to have on your team when you need courage. It also requires faith and Mary – mother of Jesus – can surely help with that.

"Curly," said Peter in his most captainy voice, "see that these boys help in the building of the house."

"Ay, ay, sir."

"Build a house?" exclaimed John.

"For the Wendy," said Curly.

"For Wendy?" John said, aghast. "Why, she is only a girl!"

"That," explained Curly, "is why we are her servants."

From JM Barrie's *Peter Pan*

Learn to Receive, Graciously

We are rich only through what we give, and poor only through what we refuse.

~ Anne-Sophie Swetchine

Are you a giver or a taker?

Don't bother answering that, it is a trick question. It's not about giving or taking, but rather giving and receiving. Either way, I bet you chose team givers. Apparently that is the team all good girls are on. We have an unfortunate aversion to receiving, which makes life harder than it has to be.

Evelet, your relationship to receiving has a profound impact on the quality of your life. Women, in particular, struggle with receiving. I once attended a talk on The Art of Receiving, and only 10 per cent of attendees were men. Despite fully appreciating the importance of receiving graciously, it is a skill I've yet to master. I prefer giving. My reluctance to receiving is about control. The way I see it, as the giver you get to call the shots; what you are giving, to whom and why. Receiving, on the other hand, has too many unknowns. Why is this being given to me? Where are the strings? It makes me feel vulnerable, an emotion I've yet to embrace fully. This block is entirely fear based. Control issues are really trust issues in a power suit.

For years I was very proud of my independence and wore it like a badge. I considered my self-sufficiency as one of my most admirable traits – until I had a baby, which quickly disabused me of the notion that I could do everything myself. Having to ask for and accept help made me realise that my independence originated from a place of fear. I was scared to need people in case they let me down. I was scared to ask for help in case I was rejected, so I learned to fulfil my own needs and ignore the ones I couldn't fulfil myself. Along the way, I spun my fear as a virtue. It is not. What takes a lot of strength is to accept that you need help and to seek it. It takes courage to be vulnerable, to say, "I need help" and then to receive it, with grace.

An aversion to receiving is not unique to me. Can you relate to any of these blocks?

• I feel unworthy of what I am being given. • I don't enjoy feeling like a charity case. • I should be able to provide for myself and not have to rely on others. • I feel obliged to give something back. • I don't like feeling as if I owe someone, so I give them back more than they gave me. • There is no such thing as a free lunch… what do they want in return? • When I give I feel in charge, but when I receive I feel inferior to the giver. • I was taught that it is better to give than to take.

This last one befuddles me. Many people erroneously believe that the converse of giving is taking, when it is actually receiving. Taking is something else entirely. Taking does not require a giver. The dance is between a giver and a receiver. Either way we have been taught that it is better to be the giver. This could not be more illogical if it were a fish on a bicycle. A giver needs a receiver. If we are all noble givers to whom are we giving? This is how we end up feeling depleted. If you give, give, give while accepting nothing in return, you eventually run on empty, crash and burn. The worst part is that it's all actually a farce.

We are covert takers. Few people give without the expectation of reciprocation, making our giving a convoluted way of taking. You may convince yourself that you are giving freely, like when you commit selfless acts for your partner, children, friends, family, even strangers until they "misbehave" and these words escape from your lips, "After all I've done for you?" Ah Evie, it turns out you were keeping score all along. Occasionally I let another driver cut in front of me in traffic, I like the high I derive from my generosity, that is until the driver, who is now ahead of me, does not pay me back with the customary "thank you" gesture of a raised hand or flashing hazards. Then I drive behind them stewing, and sending them energetic poison darts. Don't be fooled and don't fool yourself, it is not giving if you expect something back for it. So how about we get off the giving high horse and embrace the art of receiving.

Learn to receive graciously – gifts, assistance, advice, support, even compliments. Receiving is the gift the recipient gives to the giver, making the act of receiving as noble as that of giving. Giving and receiving go together like breathing, you cannot exist entirely on inhales (receiving) and you will expire even quicker if all you do is exhale (giving). Learning to receive is an essential requirement for those seeking residency in the land of WOWness. Many women strive to be givers, an occupational hazard of the gender assigned the role of nurturer. Yes, nurturing is a feminine charge. Giving, however, is the domain of the masculine – making its opposite, receptivity, a feminine attribute. Look at the sexual act and the design of our genitals. The male penetrates, pushes, advances, while the female accepts, allows and contains. The masculine gives, the feminine receives. Receiving and nurturing are not mutually exclusive; in fact, they are complementary and interdependent. You will be useless at nurturing if you are depleted. Why do you think airline safety procedure insists that you place the oxygen mask on yourself first before attending to those who need help? It is the only way it can work. Asphyxiating people are in no position to save anyone. The reason so many of us are chronically drained is because we attempt to excel at nurturing while being very poor receivers. The results of this imbalance range from general crabbiness to various diseases caused by mental, physical and emotional depletion. If you accept that one of the roles of the feminine is to nurture, then logically you must acknowledge that the feminine must receive. This may seem wrong because our conditioning dictates the opposite, but look around; this isn't exactly a healthy society we live in. Be attentive whenever you come cross information that contradicts the norm; it's probably more sensible.

It is woman's role to receive, and man's to give. Yes, men are great receivers, which is why their path requires them to learn to give. In spite of being great receivers, most men innately resonate with their role as givers. Nothing emasculates a man quicker than feeling like he is not needed. Women emasculate men by not creating space to receive what men seek to give.

I was brought up to be strong and capable, and for years aspired to practising absolute self-sufficiency. A boyfriend at varsity had a car and I didn't. He'd offer to drive me home and I'd refuse. Instead, I would walk from Braamfontein to downtown Johannesburg to catch a taxi. I never understood why this offended him; I thought he'd appreciate that I was low maintenance. Another boyfriend confessed, as the credits rolled on our relationship, that I made it impossible for him to feel like a man. "Why could you not let me take care of you?" he inquired, deflated and frustrated. At the time, I failed to see what that had to do with the demise of our relationship.

Receiving isn't that difficult. It is only a "yes" away. To an offer of help say, "yes, please", whether you can handle it yourself or not, to a compliment say, "yes, thank you", instead of rebuffing it with a put-down such as, "oh no, this old thing?" You will feel good and energised. The giver will feel good. Everybody wins. Receiving places you firmly in your natural feminine state, allowing the men an opportunity to give, which is an expression of their masculine role as providers. Think back to your school days: which girls always had boys buzzing around them? The ones who said "yes".

On that note, let us talk about sex, Evie. Sex epitomises the relationship between giving and receiving. Many women's sexual experience can improve vastly by learning how to receive sexual pleasure, instead of focusing on developing skills of how to give it. A legacy of patriarchy is that women have been sold a lie about sex, which we have bought, bagged and now lug around. We've been mesmerised into believing sex isn't really our thing.

Big sexual appetite in woman = nymphomania – a psychological condition.

Big sexual appetite in man = virility.

Pursuit for sexual variety in woman = slutty.

Pursuit for sexual variety in man = studly.

What woman wants in sex = relationship.

What man wants in relationship = sex.

We've been had, bamboozled! Women, in fact, have greater sexual capacity than men. Men reach their sexual peak in their late teens to early twenties, while women only peak in their late thirties to early forties. We have an organ whose sole purpose is to give pleasure, the clitoris. That is its only job. Let that sink in, Evelicious. Eight thousand sensory nerve endings are there, purely for your sexual pleasure; and they say God is a man! Women are naturally multi-orgasmic; men have to learn to have multiple orgasms. Women's orgasms are significantly longer than men's. We score on quality and quantity. Prolactin, a biochemical produced at climax, causes men to feel sleepy after sex, and with age they require increasing recovery time between erections. Women, on the other hand, are energised by good sex. While your lover lies spent after sex, you could effortlessly bound to another one for more sexual acrobatics.

Hang on while I wait for lightening to strike me down.

Nothing?

Okay.

Our crafty forefathers were effective in brainwashing us into believing that sex is a guy thing. Only a few hundred years ago mothers were advising their newlywed daughters to just grin and bear it. "Lie back and think of England," the Victorians soothingly told their daughters. We have come some way since, but it is still not yet *uhuru*. We haven't really become sexually liberated as much as we have become more sexualised. We have evolved from being passive sexual objects for the pleasure of men – open your legs and think of England – to being active sexual objects for the pleasure of men. Take pole dancing classes, perfect a strip tease, rock a pair of crotch-less panties, sport a Brazilian, learn how to blow his mind with a blow job. The pleasure of the man is supreme. Young women, weaned on music videos and googled porn think they have to perform for men. Women, hypnotised by movies, fear that a "normal" woman has an earth-shattering orgasm within three minutes of being in the general vicinity of an erect penis. If you are not "normal" rather fake it than bruise his big, but brittle, masculine ego.

The very nature of the sex act is receptive for women. Whether a man is using his penis, fingers or tongue, you receive him into your body. We receive physically, but not necessarily emotionally or energetically. The same goes for men, their physiology demonstrates their role as givers of pleasure, but emotionally, energetically and psychologically, many are sexual takers. That is how both genders are socialised; women to give, men to get or take – depending on the man's moral compass.

When I broach this subject with women, predictably, it generally does not go down well. I couldn't resist that pun. "Liberal" women don't like the idea that we traded one form of sexual slavery for another, so our first reaction is to deny or defend our state. One friend countered that, like men, occasionally she, too, has sex in which she is the taker. Although this appears liberated and progressive, true liberation and bravery would be a 100 per cent receptive state – free of the fear to perform, free of the need to come across as a great lay, free of the need to be the boss of his orgasms. As I've pointed out, taking does not require a giver, receiving does. As such, receiving requires a greater sense of self-worth than taking. It implies that you are worthy of someone else wanting to give to you.

Are you, Evelet?

Can you imagine taking on that sexual role without feeling pangs of panic? Receiving requires openness, honesty and vulnerability, states most of us fear. There are layers of multi-generational fear, trauma, shame and guilt carried within our feminine loins. So be gentle with yourself and take baby steps. The next time you have sex with someone you trust, who is capable of creating a safe emotional space for you, open up and allow yourself to just receive... and remember to breathe through all the panic and conditioned need to perform.

Given half a chance, men thrive as bringers of your sexual pleasure. With time, men appreciate the gift you give them when you become the receiver. Allow yourself to be comforted by the words of David Deida,[22] "Usually my body is something I use – to work, to play, to get things done. But when I feel your body opening to mine, my body remembers love. Your sexual surrender awakens me to a depth of love I rarely feel in my body any other time of the day... Your pleasure of surrender blesses my life and opens me in ways that feel new and deeper every time we make love." Evie, I am not saying you are never to be the giver – I would hate to be responsible for dropping the country's fellatio rate – but that has never been your problem, has it? Your challenge is to learn to bask in the energy of receiving, with grace.

A goddess masters the art of deliciously savouring a juicy compliment or gift, and fearlessly accepting an offer of service. When someone tells you that you look good in those jeans, you are to thank them with a radiant smile, and give them a slow twirl so they can really see how fabulously you rock them jeans. Don't rush out of the moment with an awkward acknowledgement or rebuttal, before deftly changing the subject. I had a nice jacket I'd bought to wear to a wedding, but it wasn't really my style. Occasionally I'd wear it to work. A colleague commented that it was a lovely jacket. She seemed really enamoured by it, so I offered it to her. Within a split second of accepting the jacket she had bailed out of that moment and was fretting about how she should reciprocate. She worried, aloud, "Now I have to find something to give you." I didn't give her the jacket because I wanted something back for it, I gave it to her because I didn't care for it and she appeared to really like it. What was meant to be a nice feel-good moment for us both became awkward instead, as she fretted and I tried to soothe her with assurances that I expected nothing in return.

Blocks to receiving will cause you to miss out on a lot of growth and bounty. Listening, for instance, is a form of receiving and when you are a bad listener you miss out on valuable information, guidance and constructive feedback. If you cannot listen you will not hear the yearnings of your heart and the guidance of your intuition. Many of us are atrocious listeners. In conversation, our silence is seldom an indication of attentive listening. It usually means we are waiting for our turn to speak or we are thinking about what we are going to say when it is our turn – that is, when we are not interrupting the person we should be listening to. Personally, I can't stand people who speak while I'm interrupting.

A vital part of being a good receiver is learning to ask. Do you know what you want? Can you ask for it? Are you comfortable with your desires or do you judge them as too selfish, frivolous, immature, unattainable, immoral, abnormal, ambitious or not what you should want? Embrace your desires. Desires are the mother of creation. Without desire, nothing would come into existence. Your very existence is due to Spirit's desire to experience itself. Desire begets everything. First you must want.

Work through your fear of telling people what you want. Work through your fear of wanting what you want. Free your desires. It is they that draw to you the WOWness you crave.

Do you pray, Evelet? Is there something that you have been praying for, for years and you still have not received it? Consider for a second that it has been given, even repeatedly, and you don't have it because you don't know how to receive it.

"Ask and it shall be given."

Generally, Spirit does not tend to do personal deliveries, your prayers, wishes and requests are often delivered through other people, so when you say "no" to help, offers and opportunities, you may be turning down the very things you prayed for. It's like the story of the religious man who escaped a flood by climbing on a rooftop and getting stranded. When a man comes by in a boat and asks the trapped man to jump in, he replies, "Go, don't worry about me, I have prayed to God for a miracle and he will save me." As the water rises to his waist another boat comes by, again he turns down the help, insisting that God will grant him a miracle. When the water is neck high, a helicopter flies by and throws down a ladder for him to escape his watery grave. Again, he declines the help. Soon enough he drowns. He arrives at the Pearly Gates a broken man and says to St Peter, "Despite being His faithful servant my entire life, when I prayed for a miracle to spare my life, God let me down." St Peter looked at him, aghast, "Dude, we sent you two boats and a helicopter!"

To be a goddess, comfortable to be served by man and Spirit, you must learn to ask and to receive. Does the idea of being served by man make you uncomfortable? How about God(dess)?

You are a goddess, Evelet, it is your divine birthright to be served by the universe through all that is in it. As Max Ehrmann wrote so insightfully in "Desiderata", "You are a child of the universe, no less than the trees and the stars." Believe it.

Becoming a Goddess: Learning to Receive with Grace

64. Examine your relationship with receiving. What limiting beliefs do you have regarding receiving? How do you take compliments and unsolicited offers of help? Are you comfortable receiving from some people and not others, or in certain situations and not others? What are your personal rules around receiving? Do you feel the need to reciprocate?

65. Learn to listen and hear. There are many books, workshops and online articles on listening. Deciding to become a better

listener is not good enough, listening is a skill you can and should learn.

a. A quick listening tip: When you find that, instead of listening during a conversation, you are busy thinking about what you are going to say next, move your consciousness from your mind into your womb. Yes, your womb. Imagine that you are breathing in and out through your womb. This shift automatically puts you in a more receptive state.

66. How do you feel about asking for help? Repeat the exercise in point 64, examining your attitude around asking for help.

67. Embrace your desires.

a. Make peace with all your desires, you have them for a good reason.

b. Allow yourself to believe that everything that you want, wants you too.

c. Out your desires. Write out a list of your desires and put them where others can see them. You can start by first putting them up on a website such as www.43things.com which will give you some anonymity. When you are braver you can maybe put them on the fridge. Desires that you put out generally find their way to fulfilment more quickly than hidden ones.

68. Meditate. Meditation teaches you to silence your mind so you can hear the wisdom of your intuition. Think of it this way: praying is talking to Spirit; meditating is listening to Spirit. You won't necessarily receive answers during meditation, but by meditating you create space and ability to receive that guidance.

69. Learn to locate your emotions within your body. Use the "How Do I Feel?" reminders from Session 7 whenever you check into your emotions and identify where in your body you feel them. When you are angry, how does your body react?

Do you clench your jaw and fists? Is your fear located in your throat, or does it feel like a twisting fist in your solar plexus? When you become an expert in reading your emotions using the feelings in your body, you will be in a better position to receive information from your body and your intuition – and to discern the difference between feelings from your fear-based ego and your intuition.

70. Divine Intervention: Identify what your barrier is to receiving and go through the goddess crew on page 231 to identify the appropriate goddess to help you shift it.

Say "Yes!" to Pleasure

> All our Western thought is founded on this repulsive pretence that pain is the proper price of any good thing.
>
> ~ Rebecca West

Evelet, are you bearing a cross?

A ten-year-old was struggling with fifth grade mathematics. His parents had tried everything: extra-classes, private tutors, Kumon, rewards, punishments, you name it. Nothing worked. Finally, despite not having set foot in a church since their wedding, they took their son to a Catholic boarding school a friend had recommended. At the end of the term, the son came home with his report card. Unopened, he dropped the envelope on the dining room table and headed straight to his room. Petrified, the parents just stared at the envelope, trying to divine what lay inside. Eventually the mother grabbed it and ripped it open. To her amazement the report had a big capital "A" next to Mathematics.

The two rushed to their son's bedroom, thrilled at this remarkable progress in a single term. "It's staying at boarding school that turned you around, isn't it?" his father asked. They boy shook his head, and said "No." "Was it the nuns?" asked the mom. Again the boy replied in the negative. "The textbooks, the teachers, the curriculum?" inquired the dad. The boy shook his head. "It must have been peer influence," concluded the mom, "The kids at these schools work hard."

"Nope," countered the son, "It happened on the very first day of school."

"What?" asked his mother.

"When I walked into the foyer and I saw that guy they'd nailed to the plus sign, I knew these people take maths very seriously."

That is one powerful plus sign. I, too, grew up in a Catholic household and the guy nailed to the plus sign, with blood seeping from his hands, feet, pierced rib and thorn-crowned forehead, could be seen in his state of eternal suffering in various high-profile locations in my home and church. This was a constant reminder that Jesus died for our sins – a vicious, cruel and protracted death. Crosses perpetually remind us that: "For God so loved the world that he gave his only begotten son." Our blessings are due to Jesus' suffering and God's great sacrifice. What great PR for suffering! Pain is redeeming. Anguish is noble. Sign me up for a spot of martyrdom. These appear to be our beliefs. We worship at the altar of suffering, reciting our mantras: "no pain, no gain", "too good to be true", "life's a bitch and then you die", "all good things come to an end", "love hurts".

Evelet, we are all nailed to the plus sign. This powerful story has set up suffering as virtuous, yet if we believe that Jesus died so we can live, happily, are we not doing the poor guy a disservice by continuing his suffering? Are we not nullifying his ordeal?

The way of the goddess is a path of pleasure, not pain – of pleasure, passion and purpose. If you are averse to embracing pleasure and joy, if you can only tolerate bliss in drops rather than floods, you won't survive the land of WOWness. We'd love to have you there, so allow me to make a case for pleasure.

Dr Christine Northrup, a leading women's health expert and author of three *New York Times* bestsellers asserts, "Pleasure is an essential nutrient that you need, each and every day, to become and remain healthy." As the accomplished Dr Northrup affirms, "Pleasure is essential." This means it is not a luxury. It is not a reward. You don't have to go through a horrible day first in order to earn it. It is also not a treat for special occasions. It does not have to be your anniversary, birthday or Women's Day for you to give yourself some Vitamin P. You should be taking a daily dose of it.

Pleasure. Joy. Bliss. Enjoyment. Delight. Ecstasy. Rapture. Glee is a daily must-have for your wellbeing. What makes Pleasure essential to your health? One of the reasons is a chemical called nitric oxide, which is released by the walls of our blood vessels. Nitric oxide is like a magic elixir because it:

• Assists the immune system to fight off bacteria
• Regulates blood pressure
• Reduces cellular inflammation, which is the underlying cause of virtually all chronic dis-ease
• Improves sleep quality
• Increases endurance and strength
• Improves wound healing
• Prevents blood clots

Nitric oxide is clearly crucial in maintaining physical health, and obviously a deteriorating body makes pleasure a challenge, but that is not why nitric oxide has a starring role in our case for pleasure. When you experience pleasure, your body releases nitric oxide. Do you get that, Evelet? There is a causal link between pleasure and physical health. Nitric oxide is essential for various crucial bodily processes and feeling good releases nitric oxide. There you go. Pleasure is essential in becoming and remaining healthy. As if that were not enough, high levels of nitric oxide trigger the release of feel-good chemicals such as serotonin, dopamine and beta-endorphins. This means that pleasure makes you feel better physically and emotionally.

Evie, do you feel guilty when you indulge in pleasurable pursuits without a "good" reason, yet happily do pleasurable things for others without an ounce of guilt? In our society, doing good is more valuable than feeling good. A high you acquire from spending the day reading books to the aged socially trumps one gained from a day indulging yourself in luxurious treatments at a beauty spa. A few years back when Iman, the Somalian supermodel, was in South Africa to launch her cosmetics range she said, "When women feel good, they do good." Perhaps she made this statement because she wanted to sell cosmetics, but being an accomplished and committed philanthropist she probably made it because she has experienced it as truth. Doing good does feel good, but it is not the recommended starting point for women. When women do good in order to feel good we often end up burnt-out or resentful.

An ebook by Sam Geppi, entitled *Stellar Relationships*,[23] explains this phenomenon using Vedic Astrology and the four elements – Earth, Water, Air and Fire. It demonstrates that, for women, feelings precede actions. When women feel good about themselves they are inclined to do good. Think about it, when you are down in the dumps you don't even want to get out of your pyjamas. On the other hand, when you feel good – say you are feeling beautiful, loved and appreciated – you are inclined towards actions that spread the joy. When we feel loved we want to spread the love. With men, on the other hand, actions precede feelings. A man who can't do good – say for example one who can't protect and provide for his family – will feel miserable and emasculated. Men use actions to feel good. Even when you feel bad they want to know what they can *do* for you.

Women's good feelings inspire good actions, but we have been pursuing emotional fulfilment in a masculine way, starting with actions instead of feelings. The feminine way appears selfish and wasteful. Through cultivating pleasure, a woman will discover her passions. Her passions will lead to her purpose and provide the impetus to fulfil that purpose. Purpose is always about service, thus the feminine pursuit of pleasure could not be further from selfish and frivolous.

This connection between pleasure and purpose unfolds beautifully in the movie *Julie and Julia*, based on the true-life stories of two unrelated American women who were born 61 years apart. The first is Julia Child, a formidable woman who left an impressive legacy. She was a chef, author and TV personality renowned for making French cuisine accessible to American housewives through her books, TV cooking shows and The American Institute of Wine & Food. Julia never set out to be anything remarkable; she did not seek the fame and fortune she ended up with. She was a bored housewife in a foreign country, France, when her husband encouraged her to find something to keep her busy. He asked her what she liked to do and her response was, "I love to eat." So she decided to take cooking classes. Pursuing her pleasure for food uncovered a passion for cooking. She immersed herself in this new-found passion and ended up writing her first cook book, which led to more books, then TV and an overall juicy, purposeful life filled with pleasure and powered by her passion for food.

Julie Powell, on the other hand, was a frustrated writer who held jobs that had nothing to do with her passion, just to pay the bills. She decided to start the Julie/Julia Project to get herself out of her emotional rut. This project entailed cooking the 524 recipes in Julia Child's first book, *Mastering the Art of French Cooking*, in 365 days and blogging about it. Julie loved cooking and she loved writing, making the Julie/Julia Project a potent combination of two things she loved. Her blog attracted a huge following, and then the attention of a publisher who offered her a book deal, which was what she had been longing for all along! Once she invested her energy in what felt good, what she wanted came to her! This movie is a wonderful demonstration of the underrated benefits of following your bliss.

The late Joseph Campbell,[24] professor and author of mythology, implored his students, "Follow your bliss. If you do follow your bliss, you put yourself on a kind of track that has been there all the while waiting for you, and the life you ought to be living is the one you are living. When you can see that, you begin to meet people who are in the field of your bliss, and they open doors for you. I say follow your bliss and don't be afraid, and doors will open where you didn't know they were going to be."

Is it getting easier for you to conceive of making pleasure a top priority in your life, Evie? Perhaps this will help: your pleasure is beneficial to others and you don't actually need to do anything for anyone in order for them to reap the rewards. A study, conducted by scientists James Fowler and Nicholas Christakis, called "Dynamic spread of happiness in a large social network",[25] revealed that happiness is catching. The study looked at the happiness of nearly 5 000 people over a period of 20 years and found that one person's happiness triggers a ripple effect that benefits not only their friends, but their friends' friends and their friends' friends' friends! Your joy is not only good for your physical and emotional health, it helps you find your purpose and it contributes to the happiness of your social network. I think the case for pleasure has been made, Evie.

However, just in case you are firmly nailed to the plus sign, I'll throw in an extra benefit to pry you loose: delight makes you light. Dr Joe Vitale,[26] famous for being one of the major contributors to *The Secret*, insists that happy people burn more calories than depressed or angry people. He lost more than 30 kilograms by focusing his attention, thoughts and actions on things that brought him joy. Think about it, when you are feeling good and filling your life with activities you love you are unlikely to be vegetating on the couch stuffing your face. Conversely, we could postulate that misery makes you fat. When we feel low we tend to self-medicate with high-fat foods, refined carbohydrate combos and alcohol, which are all high-calorie foods.

We are taught that pleasure is generally a wasteful indulgence. We are warned that pleasure is frivolous, risky and unproductive, making its pursuit a guilt-laden activity. As women, we are socialised to put the needs of others before our own and, when we put ourselves first, we are selfish. We stand accused of being unfit mothers and prodigal daughters. We perpetuate this legacy by mesmerising our impressionable daughters through fairy tale after fairy tale in which bliss can only be trusted if it is preceded by profound suffering. You must survive the evil stepmother's plot to poison you before you get to live happily ever after. You have to spend years scrubbing floors, being mistreated by your stepsisters, before you can become a princess. Only if you get abandoned in the woods and survive a cannibalistic witch, will it be okay for you to come upon good fortune.

We have all bought into it so much that we get angry with the people who break the rules. Don't we just hate trust fund babies who can spend their entire lives doing only what they like? Especially if they unashamedly choose to make the pursuit of pleasure their primary occupation. If anyone could do with a good crucifying, it's Paris Hilton. How dare she just have fun all the time; living for celebrity parties, beach holidays and the attention of rich men? I bet you'd do some good with all that time and money, wouldn't you Evie? Don't get me started on Kim Kardashian. How dare she break the "no pain, no gain" rule? No one should be allowed to become a multi-millionaire from making a sex tape, that's not hard, it's not painful either if you are doing it right – unless you want it to be!

Yet, modern sages such as Joseph Campbell and Deepak Chopra teach that hard work, struggle and frustration don't gain you any spiritual brownie points; hardships actually indicate that you are out of sync with the universe. Otherwise you would be able to efficiently and effortlessly co-create with Spirit. Dare I say, your fortune may just be one sex tape away. Chopra defines success as our ability to fulfil our desires with effortless ease. Follow your bliss, implores Campbell.

A few years back, I attended the inaugural TEDxSoweto, where a young graphic designer and lecturer named Khaya Mtshali spoke about what art had taught him about life. He put up a slide that read, EMOTION IS INFORMATION, and I got goosebumps. Khaya elaborated, "When I am feeling joy about something, I know I'm doing the right things. When I am feeling low, I know

I'm doing the wrong thing and need to stop."

Imagine that.

Becoming a Goddess: Saying Yes to Pleasure

71. Do a pleasure audit. Make a list of all the things, people and places that make you feel good. Cast back to the last week, month and year. How often do you indulge in these activities? How often do you go to these places? How often do you spend time with these people?

72. Make a list of simple pleasures that require low resources. Post it on The Goddess Academy Facebook group to share it with your pleasure-starved sisters. Here are some examples:
    a. Flirting with an unlikely stranger – like a really old man or a sweaty construction guy.
    b. Splashing puddles after it rains; heck, dancing in the rain.
    c. Playing in the park like a kid; even better, playing in the park with a kid.
    d. Taking the scenic route.
    e. Finding a good spot to watch a sunset and having a picnic.
    f. Meeting up with a friend who makes you laugh out loud.
    g. Running through a sprinkler.
    h. Taking a long and luxurious bubble bath.
    i. Hiring a DVD of a musical, putting on the sub-titles and singing along.
    j. Having a pyjama party with your girlfriends, doing each other's hair and nails and talking about boys, as if you are in high school.

73. Allocate a daily minimum of three minutes for your personal delight. Three minutes is really short, in fact it is the average length of a song. Perhaps you can use it to shake your booty to a cheesy song. I love Queen songs for a quick pleasure boost.

74. Take responsibility for your pleasure. Think of ways to make any situation more fun. Play boardroom bingo at those dreaded full-day workshops where people drone on and on, trying to sound intelligent. When old people poke you in the ribs at a family event and say, "Shouldn't we be attending your wedding soon?" smile, poke them back and say, "Shouldn't we be attending your funeral soon?"

75. Hire a pleasure police. Get a friend to check up on you daily and find out if you took your dose of Vitamin P.

76. Must watch: *Julie and Julia*.

77. Divine Inspiration: Bast, Egyptian goddess of play, pleasure and parties will happily initiate you in the ways of pleasure, passion and fun.

Travel Light

If my hands are fully occupied in holding on to something, I can neither give nor receive.

~ Dorothee Solle

How much baggage do you lug around, Evie?

There is a broad-leafed tropical tree in my garden that always looks utterly pathetic in winter. Its giant leaves turn brown before they shrivel up into pitiful little stalks and break off. Each winter I mourn it, convinced that it won't survive the unforgivingly dry and cold highveld winter. Yet each year, without fail, by September it has grown significantly taller and more luscious than before. I stress about its survival, but a little less each winter.

Miss B was horrified when she found out that she must lose her teeth someday. I had to explain to her that her milk teeth – which she tends to with great commitment, limiting her intake of sweets and brushing twice a day – must fall out in order to make room

128

for new, bigger ones. She spent an entire day walking around with a hand clasped over her mouth.

It seems that life constantly requires that we let go of something for growth. Gardeners prune plants to stimulate growth, snakes shed their skin to accommodate growth spurts, children lose their milk teeth to make way for their adult teeth. Letting go might be an intrinsic part of life, but it certainly hasn't been easy for me. I wrote a letter to myself about it, which I read when I need some coaching on the subject:

Kagiso, you have never really been a hoarder of things, you release those easily as you outgrow them. Have you noticed how quickly they are replaced? You never have a shortage of things. I bet you think you release material things effortlessly because you have so many, but I am here to tell you that you have an abundance of things because you let go of them so readily. As the saying goes, nature abhors a vacuum. As such, the best way to attract new things into your life is to create space for them. You seem to have got this one intuitively, when it comes to material objects. What I would like you to do is apply the same concept to the immaterial.

You love to learn; well, learning requires acceptance of new ideas. It's hard to grow while hanging on to old beliefs and ideas. Learning is much harder when you are invested in being right. It is okay for you to let go of your old truths to embrace new ones. I know you hate being wrong. Embracing a new truth does not make the old one wrong. What if you look at it this way? Truth is relative. It is all about perspective. For example: what is a chrysalis, the beginning or the end? If you are a caterpillar it is the end, if you are a butterfly it is the beginning.

You should also consider letting go of expectations of how things should be. Often, you become unhappy because a situation, person or relationship is not conforming to your expectations. It is easier to let go of your own expectations and accept that things are as they are than fight reality in an attempt to get it to conform to your idea of how things should be. This will greatly reduce the stress and tension in your life.

While you are at it, let go of hurts too. I am about to use the F-word, forgive. They say refusal to forgive is the poison you take, hoping to kill another. I know that some things are hard to forgive, some people even seem unforgivable, but you forgive for yourself, not another. Forgiving allows you to move on. It is about letting go of hurts that occurred at a point in the past. As long as you hold on to the hurt, a part of you has to remain in that place in time with it. As soon as you forgive you call it into the present, where all of you should be. The beauty of forgiving is that you don't need to know how to do it. All you need to do is be willing to forgive. If that is still too hard to do, be willing to be willing to forgive. Soon you will get the hang of it. Then I am going to ask you to do something even harder. Forgive yourself. In every single situation that you need to forgive another you also have to forgive yourself. There is always a part of you that blames you for the experience, a part that believes you could have done something differently. Forgiving yourself sets you free. You will be free from the painful memory, and you will also be free to benefit from the lesson contained in the experience. Often, once you stop focusing on what went wrong, you notice what went right.

Finally, let go and let God. Have faith in abundance. Remember, at the beginning of this letter I commended you on your ability to let go of physical things. It is because you have faith that there is more, better stuff out there to take the place of the things you are releasing. If you applied the same faith to all other aspects of life you will let go of beliefs, situations and relationships with the same levity and joy with which you part with old shoes. Know that whatever you need to release, be it a job, a house or a person, it has a more suitable replacement.

This way you can live lightly, enjoying the flow of the river of life without the need to build any dams to hold on to the water.

There are two TV shows I watch with horror and fascination: *Clean House* and *Hoarders*. They are about people who have made their lives untenable by hanging on to literally everything they get their hands on. These people have rooms in their homes they cannot enter anymore because they are full of things. One episode of *Hoarders* had a guy who showered at the gym because he could no longer access his bathroom. It was full of rubbish. They bring in experts to help these people let go of this junk and stop bringing more home. The team obviously includes cleaners and organisers, but there is also always someone who is there to deal with the internal imbalance driving the behaviour. One woman became a hoarder after her infant child died. She had a hole on the inside that she was trying to fill up with things on the outside. Only after relentless probing did she even make the connection between her behaviour and the loss of her baby. The Universal Law of Correspondence is very instructive in this case: As within, so without. Your outer world is always a reflection of your inner world.

Once, while visiting a friend at work, I discovered that she hoards folders. Those horrid, branded ones made of canvas or faux leather, which you get at conferences and workshops. She has a mountain of them. She justified her stash by claiming that you never know when you'll need one, or 20 in her case. I began to notice that she is quite the collector of unnecessary things, for instance she'll accept the table centrepiece at the end of a wedding or function, or some other useless thing. Always with the same justification, "You never know when it might come in handy." My friend grew up in extreme poverty and, despite having done very well since, a part of her believes that there is never enough. This belief is evident in her life. She has a decent job and is married to a wealthy man, but she always needs more money than she has. Her car will break down in between insurances and it will require R80 000 to fix. The geyser will burst and somehow the damage won't be covered by her insurance. There is just never enough, and so she hangs on to folders and second-hand bouquets, when what she needs to do is let go of a belief that there is never enough.

Like the tree that sheds its leaves each winter, only by letting go of the past can you experience a new beginning. Otherwise you drag yesterday into all of your todays. Holding on to old issues – fear, anger, hurts, beliefs, guilt – is like having a ball and chain around your ankle. Not only does it make it hard for you to keep moving but you can only get so far. Psychologist Chuck Spezzano[27] teaches that holding on reflects a fear of life and taking the next step. Letting go frees you. It takes you out of the place you have been stuck and moves you forward in flow and confidence.

What does your clutter do for you, Evelet? I doubt that you have a problem that would make it on to *Clean House* but you may have a cluttered office, closet, car, garage, or drawers. Clutter is anything you no longer use or love. That stuff that you liked a decade ago when your taste was different. Those piles of old mail, newspapers and magazines are clutter. The pots of old dried paint in the garage and the pile of old ice-cream tubs in the kitchen cupboard. All of these things are clutter. Declutter your life and pay attention to the emotional holes and deep-seated beliefs you upset as you remove their external crutches.

Clutter is not all physical, but it always takes up space. If you are struggling to bring things into your life, you may have energetic clutter taking up room. Perhaps on some level you are still holding on to that relationship from way back, and this is why you haven't quite succeeded in sustaining another decent relationship. Believe it or not, when you truly let go, something better always comes to take the place of what you let go. You can end a relationship, chuck the ring at him, pack your bags and move out, but if you are still cyber-stalking him, if you compare all subsequent suitors to him (positively or negatively), if you obsess over his new life, you are still holding on and hence won't have space for a new love. Letting go gives you back your power. This is one of the things that make forgiveness such a powerful choice. Forgiveness frees you from the past and restores your power. Holding on binds you to where you were, making you unavailable to present life and its presents. Let go by forgiving – others and yourself. In NLP (Neuro Linguistic Programming) there is a saying that people are always doing the best they can with the resources they have available. This includes you. Look at the situations you regret and ask yourself: in that moment, were you not doing the best you could with your available physical, emotional, mental and spiritual resources? You may be in a different place now, with a different set of resources that enable you to make a different choice, but I bet at the time you did the best you could. If there was ever a secret to a happy, healthy life it is learning to forgive. Forgiveness is the technique that Dr Ihaleakala Hew Len used to cure the criminally insane patients we spoke about in Session 5. As he was looking at the pictures of the patients, he repeated the following phrase, "I am sorry, and I love you". That's it, love and forgiveness. If Dr Len can cure a ward full of criminally insane people, whom he has never met, through love and forgiveness, imagine what you can do in your own life. In almost all religions and ancient philosophies, forgiveness is one of the keys to peace and happiness.

Anaïs Nin[28] observed, "Life is a process of becoming, a combination of states we have to go through. Where people fail is that they wish to elect a state and remain in it. This is a kind of death." When we hang on to things that no longer serve us, things from the past, we block the flow of life. The Universal Law of Flow teaches us that we live in a universe comprised of energy, which flows like a river. Nothing is static. Everything is in constant motion. What happens to a river when the flow is blocked? It overflows, causing a lot of damage or it stagnates – the water turns putrid and can no longer sustain life. The Law of Flow governs every area of your life. If a cupboard is crammed full, nothing new can be put into it. If you hoard anything, whether it is money, clothes, grudges or resentments, there is no room for new things to come in. To allow anything new in your life you must let go of the old. If you hold on to old emotions and continually re-run old memories, they will prevent fresh experiences from coming in.

Allow your river to flow by removing emotional blocks. Release all that anger buried from being bullied in primary school by punching a pillow and screaming your lungs out until that lump in your throat subsides. Release all your grudges. Forgive whoever needs forgiving, more importantly forgive yourself. When you are done, let new and better things flow into your life. Make sure that you replace the old with something better. There is no point in quitting smoking just to start stuffing yourself with food. Find a better way to fill that vacuum; don't just trade in an old problem for a new one. Don't leave the dead end job and settle for a new equally unrewarding one.

Every time you clear out, raise your standards. This is how you will find yourself firmly on the path to the land of WOWness, by travelling light.

Becoming A Goddess: Leaving Baggage Behind

78. Pick a month to declutter your life. Repeat at least once a year.

    a. Start with physical things. Go through your closets, garage, cupboards, car, and get rid of things you no longer use. Throw them away or pass them on to other people who may need them. I give all my old clothes to my grandmother's church; my friend Gilda throws clothing swap parties each year around the time of her birthday.

    b. Let go of habits that are incongruent with who you choose to be.

    c. Let go of people who do not reflect the person you choose to be. If you want to become more health conscious, the friends you shared alcoholic binges with, resulting in you needing the rest of the weekend to recover, may not fit in with your new choice to wake up at 5.00 am for a morning run.

    d. Let go of beliefs. The nice thing about the decluttering process is that it reveals issues you may not even know you had. It gives you an opportunity to discover your beliefs. If they are limiting beliefs, you can use various techniques to release them. I hung on to an engagement ring from a failed relationship for years. When I finally forced myself to part with it, I discovered that I had hung on to it for so long because I was afraid that no one else would ever find me lovable enough to get me a ring that valuable. I gave up the ring and dealt with my belief that I was unworthy.

79. Forgive. Forgive others and forgive yourself. Some people and things are easier to forgive than others.

    a. Get to a place where you can forgive. You can pray for assistance. You can tell yourself repeatedly that you are willing to be willing to forgive. You can use EFT on your unwillingness to forgive.

    b. Find a process to support your intention to forgive. One simple but powerful exercise is to do the following: Every day for a week, each day, write, "I (fill in your name), forgive (fill in a person, place or thing) completely." Write this 70 times. For example, "I Kagiso, forgive God completely." The next week, repeat the exercise, writing, "I (your name), forgive myself completely" – 70 times. At the end of the 14 days take all that paper and burn it while offering a little prayer or intention to free yourself from the past.

80. Good to read:

    a. *Radical Forgiveness: A revolutionary five-stage process to heal relationships, let go of anger and blame, find peace in any situation* by Colin Tipping is a great book on forgiveness. It has a step-by-step worksheet to walk you through the emotional and psychological steps of forgiveness.

    b. *Zero Limits: The Secret Hawaiian System for Wealth, Health, Peace, and More* by Joe Vitale and Ihaleakala Hew Len.

81. Divine Intervention: Chinese goddess Kuan Yin helps people feel compassion and mercy towards themselves and others. Ask her for support in your efforts to forgive. Welsh moon goddess Cerridwen and Hindu goddess Kali are both associated with death and birth, making them perfect teachers in your quest to release the old to make way for the new.

Mind Your Language

Handle them carefully, for words have more power
than atom bombs.

~ Pearl Strachan

What are you sorry for, Evie?

"The day I'm having!

"Girl, sit down, this might take a while. I had a puncture in
morning traffic, in the rain. Only to discover that Thabang didn't
renew our AA membership, he is so unreliable these days, and
nobody stops to help anymore in this town. It was raining cats and
dogs, and I was drenched. I looked like a wet cat, and my braids
smell like one, still. I only managed to get to work at noon, and
you'd think it would have killed dragon boss lady to show some
sympathy. Now Miss B's brought a note home; her teacher wants

to see me for some reason. It doesn't sound good. Anyway Hon, how are you doing?"

Men bond over sport, using short sentences. Women, we bond by sharing personal stories, in really long monologues. Nothing wrong with it, that's just how we do. If you pay attention you'll notice that our tendency is to tell negative stories. We prefer to talk about our misfortunes, suffering, inadequacies and fears instead of our victories, strengths, joys and fortunes. We call it exhaling. A more descriptive term for it is wound bonding. We bond over our wounds, like soldiers sharing war stories. We even get competitive. "Your thighs look like cottage cheese? Girl, please, mine look like I was caught in a hail storm." We just love wound bonding. Sometimes, in the midst of a misadventure, we get a rush just thinking about how and who we are going to regale with the story of our misfortune.

Think about the last time something good happened to you, like a nice romantic surprise or a genuine compliment from your hypercritical boss. How many people did you tell? Three, tops? The last time something bad happened to you, not even something major, say your domestic helper used two bottles of extra virgin, extra expensive olive oil to make fat cakes, how many people did you share that story with? I bet you told anyone who cared to listen.

Exhaling makes us feel better, that is why we do it. When women talk about their problems, our brains release serotonin, nature's "feel good" chemical. Which is why talking about something makes us feel better, calmer and less stressed out. Incidentally, it doesn't work the same for men – so don't insist that he talks it out; he deals with his issues by retreating.

Alas, our talking about issues is a double-edged sword. Although I know how good exhaling sessions feel, I would like to ask you to put some limits to them. Energy follows attention. Where attention goes energy flows and wherever energy flows stuff grows. Essentially, whatever you give your attention to, you get more of. Stories are attention magnets; they are fed by the energy of the narrator, as well as the attention of the audience, and with wound bonding the audience tends to be wide. In his book *The Four Agreements*,[29] a book of ancient Toltec wisdom presented as four agreements to make with yourself for a fulfilling life, author Don Miguel Ruiz advises that you limit your exhaling session to three accounts. That is, tell your story a maximum of three times and then let it go. I've become quite strategic with my selection of three. I tend to save the first account for someone who will let me complain and moan, and even get angry with me. My friend Sindi is great at this. She literally gets pissed off right along with you. I save the last for someone who will yank me out of victim mode – usually a man because they generally aren't too comfortable with just listening to problems without diving in to "fix" them – or my friend Gilda who can find the silver lining in the most menacing of clouds.

Once you implement the three accounts rule you'll be shocked by how much wound bonding you used to do. This limit will put a heavy dent on your conversation content. Why, you may wonder, is this woman raining on my moaning parade? Because your words are very powerful, that's why. You create with the words you utter. Whatever you speak about you get more of. Whatever you speak about you become. Whatever you speak about you realise. I know how to give myself a bad flu, and it does not involve licking the escalator handrail at the mall. I made you gag, didn't I? I just need to consistently complain about being tired for a week or two and then *bam!* I am floored by a virus, which ensures that I have to stay in bed for a few days. I must admit, sometimes this happens to me – talking myself into a case of flu – other times I do it wilfully. If, for whatever reason, I feel a need to rest but I don't see how I can find the time, I give myself the flu, literally by complaining about how tired I am. I once created two tyre punctures with my words. It was rainy season and I kept on telling people that my tyres were due for a change. Since I had neither the time nor inclination to change them, all I did was talk, and talk and talk about how worn out my tyres were and how unsafe this made my car, without making any attempt to fix the issue. Soon I drove over some nails that were scattered on the road, got two punctures and had to change my tyres. I am a sorceress, casting spells with words, it seems. So are you, Evelet.

In *The Four Agreements*, the very first agreement the author urges you to make with yourself is to be impeccable with your word. This is because your word has creative power. It is your primary tool of creation. Ruiz describes the word as not just a sound but a force. The word is the power with which we think, express, communicate, and therefore affect our world. Our word influences how we feel, which impacts how we behave, this in turn affects how others react to us. Be impeccable with your word, Evie.

I once ended a friendship over a broken glass. Early in my working career I shared a townhouse with a friend from boarding school. I arrived home one evening to be told, "Your glass broke". This glass, an 18th birthday present, was very special to me. Yet she chose not to take responsibility, let alone apologise, for unintentionally breaking something that she knew had high sentimental value to me. She could just as easily have said, "I am sorry, I broke your special glass while washing the dishes." Her choice of words revealed something about her, which showed me she was not someone with whom I wanted to maintain a friendship.

I had a colleague whom I assumed was gay and once made a statement to that effect. He asked, with shock, if I thought he was gay. I responded, "Yes, aren't you?" In response he did not say, "No, I am not gay." Instead he replied, "I have a wife and two kids," which is not what I had asked him. Four years later, he stumbled out of the closet.

A wealth of information is contained in the words that people select, consciously or unconsciously. The psychological term "a Freudian slip" – a slip of the tongue where you say what you mean instead of what you meant to say – is believed to reveal what is in your subconscious. For example, when former US President George W. Bush was addressing teachers, he meant to say, "I want to thank all teachers," but "I want to spank all teachers," came out. Similarly, a male colleague once said to a well-endowed female subordinate, "I know you'll do your breast," when he intended to say "do your best". You get the drift.

While giving dating tips, the owner of a matchmaking agency advised people to listen very carefully on first dates – women, in particular, since we prefer talking to listening. He claimed that someone's true nature would reveal itself in two hours' worth of talking.

Evie, respect the word. There is one word in particular whose use I would like you to limit, especially in professional settings. The word is "sorry". In a meeting, I asked a client to pass me a bottle of water and she responded, "Oh, sorry". I asked her what she was apologising for. She gave me a blank stare, looking even sorrier for having said she is sorry. The whole exchange was so fascinating that I began to pay attention to how often people apologised for no discernible reason and I was blown away by how much women do it, especially at work.

Many women, when wanting to make a contribution in a group setting, will use the word "sorry" to get attention. Is that really how you would like to introduce your input? Even when we don't actually use the word sorry, we are extremely apologetic in our approach. For instance, nullifying the value of your questions by saying, "This is probably a stupid question..." If it is stupid then why are you asking it? If you are asking stupid questions then why are you there, using up valuable company resources and getting paid?

We complain that we are not taken seriously at work; that we are passed up for promotions, we are not given authority and our contributions are ignored. If you find that people talk over you in meetings, perhaps you have too often prefaced your input with disclaimers such as, "This is probably a stupid idea, but..." If you are unconvinced about your worth, everybody else will be too. If you act like an impostor who does not belong, others will not have any confidence in your abilities. Before you point a finger at chauvinism, favouritism, patriarchy or nepotism for a stalling career, examine the signals you are putting out about your value. There is a saying, "Sorry is as sorry does," which means that the extent of your remorse should be shown by your actions, not merely by saying sorry. Yes, actions do speak louder than words, but words affect emotions, which in turn influence actions. Stand by a mirror, look yourself in the eye and tell yourself with all the sincerity you can muster that you are sorry for being here. Notice the slump in your emotions and posture. Now repeat the exercise, except this time give yourself a genuine compliment and note the difference. In life there will be actions you need to apologise for, and you should. Just be careful to be sorry for what you have done, not who you are.

In the first book of the Christian Bible, Genesis, it says God created the world and everything in it, with the word. You, too, create your world with your word. An easy way to start creating a life of WOWness with your word is by replacing your wound bonding with happy stories of your triumphs, strengths and fortunes. I know what you are thinking, the word for that is bragging and nice girls just don't do that. It is immodest and unbecoming. Let me remind you, where attention flows, energy goes. You may be accused of being boastful, but the more you brag the more you'll have to brag about. Bragging is the turbo version of keeping a gratitude diary, a practice that forces you to focus on what you already like about your life and thus create more of that. Bragging is a far more powerful tool for increasing the good in your life. It combines the power of thought with the power of the word. At The Goddess Academy we call them "strut sessions", and we start each gathering with one. It is an opportunity for you to strut your stuff. Remember, whatever you speak about, you get more of. The word is a powerful manifestation tool.

There is a very effective conscious creation technique I learnt from NLP master practitioner and life coach Anisa Aven, called raindancing. It is named after the Native American Raindance. Whenever there was a drought the Native Americans would induce rain by performing a dance, during which they would act as if they were dancing in the rain. They would splash their feet in the puddles; they would feel the rain running down their bodies, weighing down their clothes; they would feel themselves getting soaked and taste the rain drops on their tongues. Essentially a raindance is not dancing for the rain, it is getting it to rain by dancing *in* the rain. Because like attracts like, the only way to have something is by having it. Raindancing, in conscious creation, involves talking about what you want as if you already have it, the way the Native Americans manifest rain by dancing as if it is already raining. Balobedu from Limpopo have a similar raindance called *legobathele*, which they do during times of drought.

At The Goddess Academy's conscious co-creation playshops we do manifestation raindances. When someone has a desire that they would like to manifest, we'll help them with a raindance. For instance, I will ask the person some questions about her desire in the present and past tense, forcing her to answer as if it already existed. For example, "How did it feel when the call came that you had won the account? Did you go out to celebrate afterwards? Have you changed in any way now that you are making all this money?" Usually when someone is raindancing for the first time, we won't do it for longer than 10 minutes, because they find the exercise very challenging. Often the raindancer is shaking by the time we are finished. Many people find it frightening to speak about their desires in this way – as actualised instead of in wishy, fantasy mode. This begs the question: do you really want this? If yes, do you really think you can have this? If you can't say it, you can't claim it. The same applies to secret desires. One of the main reasons we have secret desires is that we believe we won't be able to realise them, so we avoid putting them out there – all the while secretly hoping that God(dess) will surprise us by making them come true.

Pay attention to your words, Evie, and use them to build you up not break you down. While you are at it, stop gossiping. Gossiping is about focusing on another person's shortcomings in order to feel good about your shortcomings. A double-whammy of negatives! It's like saying to the universe, "Bartender may I have a shot of negativity, in fact, make it a double." Gossiping is bad for you in so many ways. For example, it calls into action the following: (1) The Law of Attraction: where attention goes energy flows and where energy flows stuff grows. (2) The Law of Reciprocity: What you give, you get back. (3) Whoever you gossip with gossips about you.

My media and marketing career involved a lot of research. Research is vital in understanding your market, its behaviour, perceptions, needs and wants. It is an expensive and often tedious process that can quickly turn into an elaborate waste of resources, until you eventually learn that it boils down to: garbage in, garbage out. For instance, you can freak out your friends by standing at the door after hosting a dinner party and asking them if they enjoyed it or not. This will provide you with a bunch of yeses and nos, which will appear insightful until you attempt to do something with that information and you discover that all you know is that six out of 10 people enjoyed the dinner party. If you had asked them what they enjoyed and what they disliked about it, you'd have useful information you could use to make the next one better. The quality of the information you receive has everything to do with the questions you ask. At times, when asked a question, I will respond by saying, "Ask me a better question so I can give you a good answer." This often takes people aback, as they never consider the quality of their queries. It ends with the response, but it starts with the question. Imagine that an oracle appeared to two people, say Adam and Eve, who desperately wanted to improve their lives and they had an opportunity to ask the oracle a question. Adam asks, "All-knowing Oracle, I am struggling to create a life I love, what am I doing wrong?" and Eve asks, "Oracle, what is the one thing I can do for maximum positive change in my life?" Which of the two, Evelet, do you think will receive the more empowering response? Adam is likely to leave with a list of things he is doing wrong, which may or may not be instructive, but I bet it will be depressing. Eve has avoided an information overload by asking for one thing, and she has focused the oracle on what she can do right as opposed to what she is doing wrong. Learn to ask empowering questions.

Words, like everything else, are energetic. They have the power to lift you up, to inspire and empower, or to bring you down. They can motivate you or give you permission to be a slacker. Let's take the word "try". When I say, "I'll try," I know it is code for "I am not committed to this and I am only likely to do it if it doesn't feel too much like hard work." Think about it, Evelet. Try is a cop-out word. It is lame and dishonest. Evelet, will you make sure the cat doesn't get into my room? – I'll try. Evie, do you think you can have the report done by Friday? – I'll try. Try is such a non-word that it actually cannot be done. You either do something and succeed, or you fail, but you cannot try to do something. Try to close this book. Don't close it, just try. The book is still either open or is now closed, which means you did close it or you did not. In the wise words of Yoda, "Do or do not do. There is no try." Other words that do you no good are "should" and "must" or "have to". They are very disempowering. They imply a lack of choice or willingness. I should quit smoking. I have to stay in this job, I am a single mother and we need the money. The vibration of that statement just brings you down. I must. I enjoy that word – because it is so unreal. There is absolutely nothing that you must do. Think of one thing that you must do Evie, one. You must breathe. Not really, only if you want to stay alive. It might appear that you don't have a choice, but you do. You must have a job if you want to earn a salary or experience, but trust me if you didn't have a job you would not spontaneously combust and turn into a heap of ashes. You are more powerful than the words you use lead you to believe. You have greater choice than the words you utter imply. "I choose to stay in this particular job doing this particular thing, even though I hate it because that is the easiest way I can think of to access money for myself and my kids" is far more honest and empowering than, "I have to stay in this job, I am a single mother and we need the money." Everything that you do in your life is by choice and you are free to choose again, differently. Even prisoners are free to choose their thoughts. These words – try, should, must, have to, maybe, hoping, probably – drain your power and erode your accountability to self. Use them sparingly.

Mind your language, Evie.

Becoming A Goddess: Using Your Words Consciously

82. Limit your "exhaling" to three accounts.

83. Make your words work for you.
    a. If you have a group of women that you get together with regularly, like a book club, start every meeting with a strut session. Brag about all the fabulous things that you have been doing, being and having. Don't cheat, like many women tend to do and brag about other people in your life. Saying "my husband got a promotion" is not a brag about you. Saying "I got a promotion" is about you. In fact practice now by writing five things you can brag about, and post them on the Goddess Academy Facebook group. I'll go first:
        i. I have nice legs.
        ii. I am writing a book.
        iii. I am a great mother.
        iv. I am very smart.
        v. I made an insanely attractive child. Yep, all me. Okay, I also knew to pick someone whose genes would support, rather than impede, the production of an über-hot offspring. So technically that's two brags – one for my genes, the other for my discerning taste in genes.
        vi. I am great at bragging.
    b. Raindance. Identify one thing that you would like to manifest, e.g., a new house, and find someone to help you raindance it. If your people are going to make you feel weird, I'll do it with you over the phone.

84. Stop starting sentences with "I'm sorry". Save it for when you are genuinely contrite about something. In fact, be super vigilant about which words you use after the phrase, "I am..." Avoid anything that you don't want to manifest.

85. Stop Gossiping.

86. Learn to ask empowering questions, even of yourself. Don't ask your beloved "Why do you like hurting me?" instead ask, "Why do you continue with this behaviour, despite knowing how it makes me feel?"

87. Avoid using disempowering words such as must, try, and should.

88. Must Read: *The Four Agreements – A Practical Guide to Personal Freedom* by Don Miguel Ruiz.

89. Divine Intervention: Call on the very sharp Athena to help you use your words more consciously.

Thou shall not consort with people who make thee feel bad about thyself. I
Thou shall cease trying to make sense out of crazy behavior. II
Thou shall not keep company with those more dysfunctional than thyself. III
Trust thy body all the days of thy life (thy mind doth fornicate with thee). IV
Thou hast permission at all times to say "NO," to change thy mind, and to express thy true feelings. V
What is not right for thee is also not right for thy brethren. VI
Thou shall not give beyond thine own capacity. VII
What thy brethren think of thee mattereth naught. VIII
Wherever thou art, therein also is the party. VIIII
Thou shall sing thine own praises all the days of thy life. X

The 10 Commandments of Self-Esteem
by Dr Catherine Cardinal

SESSION 16

Love You, More

Loving yourself... does not mean being self-absorbed or narcissistic, or disregarding others. Rather it means welcoming yourself as the most honoured guest in your own heart, a guest worthy of respect, a loveable companion.

~ Margot Anand

Think about the three people you love the most, Evie.

Did you make it onto the list?

If you are not number one on the list of people you love, you are sleeping on the job. You are doing the people who you love a disservice, because I bet you expect them to provide the love that you are not giving yourself. You are keeping your loved ones hostage, Evie.

We all need love. Human beings cannot thrive without love. Love is like oxygen for our souls. Fortunately it is abundantly available and freely accessible. That is, if you are your own source of love. Self-love = love on tap. Like oxygen, you seldom have to think about where your next hit is going to come from. Unlike oxygen, self-love needs to be cultivated.

We are born with a healthy quantity of self-love. All kids are completely in love with themselves, but this innate self-love ebbs with time as we neglect our relationship with ourselves, and internalise all the critical voices telling us that we are unworthy, unlovable, inadequate and undeserving.

It is fascinating how averse we are to self-love. Most of us would much rather focus on loving other people, and getting other people to love us, than on loving ourselves. We have all gone to great lengths to get or keep the love of another. We've all had our bunny-boiler moments, whether you actually did it, or merely thought about it, is immaterial. We have had moments of utter despair from craving the love of another. All the while we continue to ignore the truest and best source of love – ourselves. It's like taking your free source of oxygen and handing it over to someone else and saying, *"Someone, I no longer want free access to oxygen. I want you to be the boss of my oxygen. I will get my oxygen from you. Yes, this oxygen I can have anytime I please, I would much rather have you administer it to me. What would be even cooler is if you give me your oxygen supply and I become the boss of yours."*

We reject ourselves and then proceed to expend immense energy trying to secure the love of others.

"I need oxygen. I must have oxygen. Somebody help me, I can't breeeeeeeathe!"

We succeed in securing that external love; then the hard work starts. Now we have to work at keeping the love. This makes us feel insecure and we become controlling.

"Oxygen supplier must stop riding a motorbike, it is dangerous and he might die with my oxygen."

"That hood rat, Miss Thang, is eyeing my oxygen supplier. She is never setting foot in my house ever again."

"When I secured this oxygen supplier my boobs were much

perkier and my butt much tighter, does he still enjoy supplying my oxygen now that all my lady lumps are migrating south? I must keep an eye on all the perky bitches who might try to go for my supplier or maybe even get a nip and tuck."

If we are fortunate we become comfortable and secure in the love of our beloved. Then we start to notice the shortcomings in how our beloved loves us. People seldom express their love in ways that match our expectations perfectly. So we become demanding, angry or resentful. *"I've got a great supplier, but I really wish he told me more how much he loves being my oxygen supplier, like Karabo's supplier does with her.*

"I wish he'd give me a lot more oxygen in public, why is he not supplying it in front of people, is he ashamed of being my supplier? Is he trying to look like a free agent?"

This tragicomedy takes up a lot of our energy. We play it out all the time, adamantly resisting being our primary source of love. We seem to view self-love as a last resort; second-rate love for the unloved and unlovable. The love we look to when we can't get someone else to love us.

Even during this era of goddess movements and fabulosity, Oprah and Marriane Williamson, meat-free Mondays and recycling, we still prefer love from another over love of self. Occasionally we are even willing to abandon ourselves for that love. I remember catching up with a friend, who by many accounts is considered to be a self-aware and enlightened person. She had reunited with an ex she'd broken up with because they sought different levels of commitment; she wanted an exclusive relationship while he wanted the freedom to see other people. I inquired if he had changed his stance. He hadn't. Was exclusivity no longer important to her? It was, still. "So, although you want an exclusive relationship you would much rather share him than not have him at all?" I asked. Her response was that she went back because she wanted to practice unconditional love.

I can fill a page with the names of women I know personally who have used the pursuit of unconditional love to rationalise their choice to settle for a lot less than they want romantically.

I roll with the enlightenment seeking, organic foods, yoga and meditation crowd. Unconditional love is big with our kind. Due to personal experience down this "unconditional love" rabbit hole, I knew the right question to ask my friend to determine whether hers was a genuine desire for personal growth or a clever rationalisation to justify her decision to sell herself short. I asked her for an honest, heart-based response to the following question, "If you loved yourself unconditionally, would you be with him?" Her answer was a deflated, yet resolute "NO". Charity and love begin at home, Evelet.

We stay in relationships that are not worthy of us because our love for self is conditional. We love ourselves enough for someone of our looks, social standing, professional success, or bank balance. Even more tragic, how much we love ourselves depends on how much we think certain people in particular love us. We think that our lovability is determined by others, so we work hard to "make" them love us, in order to prove that we are loveable. Meanwhile, the truth is the opposite, how much we love ourselves determines how much others will love us.

Years ago I was struggling to leave a relationship. I desperately tried falling out of love with the guy, thinking this would minimise the heartbreak when the time came to end the relationship. I attempted to achieve this by focusing on all the things I hated about him. This strategy didn't make me love him any less; all it did was make me feel worse about being in the relationship. One day I had an epiphany, which I shared with him, "My problem is that I love you more than I love me, and when the day comes that I love myself more, I will leave you." The issue was not that I loved him too much; it was that I did not love myself enough. From then on I worked on cultivating self-love. I withdrew my focus from him, what he did right or wrong, what I hated or loved about him, and focused on learning to love myself. Many months later – unlike in movies this stuff takes time in real life – the day arrived when I was able to fulfil my promise.

Perhaps we default to pursuing another's affection above our own because we know ourselves too well. Knowing our light and shadow, strengths and weaknesses, virtues and vices, we may have concluded that our imperfection makes us unlovable. We can always show only our best side to others, at least for a while, but it is harder to hide from ourselves. We seek the easier love, the love from others who may never truly know all of us.

When I was 16 weeks pregnant with Miss B, because of some unfortunate mix-up, my blood tests came back indicating an extremely high risk of Down's Syndrome. The gynaecologist strongly recommended termination. After the news had sunk in, termination was definitely an option. I could have a more definitive scan, but I'd have to wait another six weeks before she was developed enough. I chose to wait for the scan and, in the interim, explored my reasons for being so resistant to having a child with Down's Syndrome. It turned out that my biggest concern was not the child's health or other possible difficulties in life. I was afraid that I wouldn't love the child, because it was imperfect. I was also afraid that others would not love me because I had an imperfect child, making me imperfect and thus unworthy of love. Until that point I did not realise that, for me, perfection was a pre-requisite to giving or receiving love. I know a lot of people who pride themselves on being perfectionists. I was one of them, but now I realise that – at least for me – it is a fault not a virtue. What is your relationship with perfection, Evie? In her book *The Gifts of Imperfection*[30] Brené Brown makes a distinction between perfectionism and self-improvement. She points out that "perfectionism is the belief that if we live perfect, look perfect, and act perfect we can minimise or avoid the pain of blame, judgement and shame... It's a 20-ton shield that we lug around thinking it will protect us when, in fact, it's the thing that's really preventing us from taking flight". When you must be perfect in all you do, sooner or later you figure out that the best way to achieve this is by doing only things you can be perfect at. This greatly limits your expression and life experience.

Thinking too much about how twisted our relationship with love has become will make your head hurt. Okay, it's making my head hurt, so here are my last words on the subject.

You cannot fall head over heels, madly in love with your life if you are not head over heels, madly in love with yourself. There is only one person in the entire world that you spend every living minute of your life with, 24/7, that person is you. Wherever you go, there you are. Whoever else you may be with, there you are. The most effective thing you can do to transform a life of OKness, even of misery, to one of WOWness, is by improving your relationship with yourself. The more you can fall for you, the better your experience of life will be. Everything feels better, looks shinier and tastes sweeter when you share it with people you love, and you share all your experiences, all the time, with you. Imagine if you really, honestly and truly dug you, Evie. You'd be floating on a cloud of WOWness around the clock.

As they say, love is a doing word, so let us look at what you can do to encourage yourself to fall for you.

Becoming A Goddess: Wooing Yourself

90.   Let your suppliers off the hook. Tell them, "I love you. I know you love me and I set you free. My sense of worth and the quality of my life are not your responsibility, but mine. You are just a fabulous cherry on top."

91.   Profess your love. Daily from today, perhaps when you are stuck in traffic, look at yourself in the mirror and say to yourself, "I love you". Say it in the first, second and third person, i.e., Kagiso, I love you; Kagiso, you love yourself; Kagiso loves herself. Do this every day until it stops feeling like a lie.

92.   Unconditional love. Learn to accept yourself – as you are. To love yourself you must accept yourself. Write a list of all the things about you that you disapprove of or feel ashamed of. Maybe you hate that you are clumsy, you wish you were thinner, or are ashamed that you were divorced by the age of

30. In front of a mirror, looking into your eyes, choose one issue and say to yourself, "I am clumsy. Evie, you are clumsy. Evie is clumsy." Repeat the phrase for at least 10 minutes. Repeat regularly until there is no emotional charge to it. While working with the one issue, do EFT on it, starting with a phrase like this: "Even though I am clumsy, and I am always tripping over myself, I deeply and completely love and accept myself." Repeat this phrase whenever you hear your inner critic admonish you for your clumsiness.

93. Forgive yourself. Write a list of all the things for which you feel guilt or regret. Take one issue at a time. Say you had an abortion that you regret or feel guilty about. (a) Work to understand why you did it. Why did it seem like your best option at the time? (b) Work to accept it. See the point above on acceptance. Identify and write out – it is important to literally write this out – the lesson you learned from the experience. Seek the gift of the experience. (c) Work to forgive yourself. Refer to session 14.

94. Take yourself out on a date. Spend time with yourself, out in public. Look good while doing it. Catch a movie and a meal, have a picnic in the park. Do not take any props. If you take anything, like a book, it should be for your pleasure, not to shield your aloneness from the world. Repeat until it stops feeling awkward.

95. Get a small book that you can keep in your handbag and start a list of 100 things you love about yourself. It will take a while to get to a hundred. When you do, throw yourself a party of 1 or a 100, but throw a party.

96. Take your daily dose of Vitamin P. Refer to session 13.

97. Check your alignment, regularly. "Happiness is when what you think, what you say and what you do are in harmony."

– Mahatma Gandhi. Ensure that your thoughts and beliefs support your highest ideal for yourself and that your actions reflect that ideal. Do you say that your relationships make you happy, but you spend most of your time at work? Most of us know the things that make us happy, but surprisingly – out of habit or obligation – we spend a lot of time doing other things that do not contribute to our happiness.

98.   Review your packaging. We use packaging to determine the value of things. If it comes in a pretty, fancy box we expect it to be far more valuable than if it comes in a plastic bag. We employ the same tactic to convey the significance of an object or experience. We'll get made up and dressed up to go to a fancy awards ceremony, but not to the garage, and we'll use fine china to serve dinner to the future in-laws but not to the neighbourhood watch. Packaging cues, conveys and evokes the appropriate level of appreciation. The *Oxford Dictionary* defines appreciation as "recognition of the value or significance of something". Do you really appreciate yourself? A goddess does not ask of another that which she is not already giving to herself. She does not expect attention from another if she does not attend to herself. She does not seek love from another if she does not love herself. She does not covet another's appreciation when she does not appreciate herself. To be appreciated by the world, you must appreciate yourself. You must recognise your value and significance.

a. Start by taking care of how you present yourself to yourself. Gather all your old, tired, discoloured and distressed undies, bid them adieu and set them alight. From now on gift-wrap yourself. Wear only underwear you would love to be seen in, especially when nobody is going to see you in it.

b. Make every day a red carpet day. Do you ever have those days where you pop in to the local supermarket in your saggy tracksuit and stretched T-shirt because there is no way you are going to bump into someone you know? And, sometimes you don't bump into anyone, other times you bump into your ex and he is not fat and his new wife looks photoshopped. Then you think it wouldn't have hurt to have taken an extra five minutes to get into a decent pair of jeans. Considering that you don't really like him, hence he is an ex, shouldn't you care when you don't look good for someone you actually like – say, you? This has several advantages: (i) It sends the right message to you about you. (ii) If you always look good for you, you'll always look good for everyone else. (iii) When you look good, you feel good. Take inspiration from my friend Lulu who says, always, and I mean always, look good, "In my world, every day is a red carpet day."

99. Detox.
   a. Detox your life of toxic people. Evaluate how everyone in your life makes you feel. Where possible, rid yourself of people who bring you down, along with friends who love you best when you are going through drama.
   b. Unplug from the "feel bad" machine. One week a month, go on a media diet. No media = no bad news about crime, natural disasters, duplicitous politicians, surgically enhanced celebrities and photoshopped models. You will feel great!
   c. Detangle from the "shoulds". Devise a plan to free yourself from all the things you do because you should. Implement it.

100. Write yourself a love letter. Get some beautiful stationery, sit down and write yourself a love letter. In it, say to yourself everything you would love to have a beloved say to you. Post the letter, via snail mail. It's great that our postal service is so unpredictable. Intend to get it back on a day you need to read those loving words.

101. Take very good care of your body. There is no getting around this. Eat healthily, exercise, rest. If you don't care for your body you cannot possibly have true love for yourself, or at least your life. If you smoke, or subsist on 2-minute noodles, really ask yourself why you are wilfully, albeit slowly, committing suicide.

102. Start a brag book. In this book, record your achievements and successes, the compliments you receive and things you appreciate about yourself – qualities, features, characteristics and skills. Make this book a constant companion. Read it when you need to remember how fabulous you are.

103. Befriend your inner critic. Although the inner voice that is constantly berating and criticising you brings you down and does you harm, it means well. Get to know your inner critic, and then gradually work on turning it into your inner cheerleader. You will soon have lots of cheerleading material from your brag book.

104. R-E-S-P-E-C-T. Respect is essential in any healthy relationship. Do you respect yourself? Examine your boundaries. Do you have boundaries? Do you uphold them? Are you consistent about how you can and cannot be treated or do you sometimes abandon yourself for others? Show yourself some respect.
      a. Never apologise for who you are. There are times that you may need to apologise for what you have done, but vow that from now on you will never, ever, apologise for who you are.

105. Trust and reliability. Trust is a cornerstone of any successful relationship. Do you trust yourself? Can you count on yourself? Strive to always keep your word to yourself and listen to your intuition.

a. What lies have you been telling yourself? Are you lying to yourself regarding how you feel about your job, body, relationship? Are you settling for less than you want? Are you settling for different from what you want? Why? Do you not feel worthy of what you want?

106. Flirt. Flirt, with everyone – strangers, babies, dogs, the elderly, men, women. Flirting is a way to use your personal magnetism to make yourself and another feel good. Make this a regular exercise.

107. Ode to your body. Acknowledge your body positively. List all the ways your body has served you in the past and continues to serve you in the present. In your dress, focus on highlighting your best assets instead of on hiding your worst. Give away all the clothes you wear when you feel fat, ugly or bloated. Refer to session 9.

108. Learn to Receive. Give yourself permission to receive all good. Accept all help, compliments, opportunities and good fortune that comes your way with a gracious thank you and a smile. Know that you deserve it. Refer to session 12.

109. Love other women. As the Universal Law of Correspondence states, "As within, so without." Generally women who don't like other women do not like themselves. Conversely you can cultivate love, acceptance and support for yourself by giving love, acceptance and support to other women.
a. Stop comparing yourself to other women. Comparison just brings you down and erodes your sense of personal power.

110. Be The One. If you were with your perfect, dream partner who treated you exactly the way you long to be treated, how would you behave? Take time to really imagine how you would be different if you were with The One. What would you be, do and have? Start incorporating those actions,

attitudes and things into your life right now because you are with The One, you are The One. Then sit back and enjoy what you see in the mirror of relationships.

111. Divine Intervention: There is no better self-love teacher than a small child. Look to the little goddesses in your life: daughters, nieces, god-daughters, cousins, neighbours... there is an endless supply of these short self-loving goddesses.

Embrace Your Femininity

> God made man stronger but not necessarily more intelligent. He gave women intuition and femininity. And, used properly, that combination easily jumbles the brain of any man I've ever met.
>
> ~ Farrah Fawcett

Daughter of Eve, are you a feminist?

An acquaintance, Byron, and I were happily conversing, when I revealed that I run a personal-development organisation for women. When I described The Goddess Academy he asked in a shocked and accusatory tone, as if I had been misrepresenting myself all along, "Are you a feminist?"

I get that often. Men point out my "feminist tendencies", reminding me of Dame Rebecca West's admission, "I myself have never been able to find out what feminism is; I only know that people call me a feminist whenever I express sentiments that differentiate me from a doormat or a prostitute." A woman has never asked me if I am a feminist; only men have. The bold or drunk ones usually then ask if I am a lesbian. "What does the one have to do with the other?" I asked in exasperation one day, and a witty male friend said, "Women." I have had numerous enlightening conversations about this, with inebriated men, through whom I learnt that to be a feminist you have to be ugly or lesbian, and not any kind of lesbian, a man-hating one. Apparently only misandrist lesbians and ugly women who can't get a man are drawn to feminism. I find that many women do not want to be labelled as feminists, perhaps because of such views.

It's a pity, because I really like the word. To me it speaks of the restoration of femininity to its rightful place of equality to masculinity. Unfortunately, in present-day lexicon, feminism has been misinterpreted to be about men – being anti-men or better than men, or just like men.

Men. Men. Men. Men. Manly men.

Thus, reluctantly, I had to say, "No, Byron, I am not a feminist."

I do what I do not because I am anti-men, but because I am pro-women and femininity. I have christened myself a womanist, stating my occupation as "Ambassador of Womanly WOWness". Will you join my womanist movement, Evie? The world – and women in particular – are in desperate need of femininity advocates.

Feminine and masculine are more than biological genders. They are energies, present in both men and women. Even though we all carry masculine and feminine energies irrespective of our gender, feminine energy has been suppressed, denigrated, demonised and demoted for thousands of years now, resulting in masculinity becoming an epidemic.

Any healthy entity – be it a person, relationship, organisation, planet, or universe – requires a balance between masculine and feminine energies. This is what is taught in the Chinese philosophy of Yin and Yang. Opposing forces are interconnected: hot-cold, night-day, wet-dry, active-passive, thinking-feeling, giving-

Yin	Yang
Female	Male
Night	Day
Passive	Active
Moon	Sun
Intuitive	Logical
Cold	Hot
Soft	Hard
Dark	Bright
Nurturing	Providing
Wet	Dry
Water	Fire
Negative charge	Positive charge
Earth	Air
Autumn & Winter	Spring & Summer
Feminine	Masculine
Emotional	Rational
Matter	Spirit
Shakti	Shiva
Being	Doing
Long-term vision	Short-term focus
Formlessness/Chaos	Structure
Passive	Active
Receptive	Penetrative
Venus	Mars
Heart	Mind
Feeling	Thinking
Unknown/Mystery	Known/Proven
Attractive	Assertive
Internal	External

receiving, being-doing, spirit-matter, male-female; they are equal, complementary and interdependent. Nothing is totally Yin or totally Yang, each contains the seed of the other. A man has feminine and masculine energies, as does a woman. Carl Jung,[31] the founder of analytical psychology, identified a man's inner woman (feminine energy) as anima, and a woman's inner man (masculine energy) as animus. For any individual to be whole and balanced, they require both feminine and masculine qualities. Feminine energy is gentle, nurturing, passive and heart-based, but a woman can put up a vicious fight, say to protect her children or secure a pair of marked-down Louboutins. Masculine energy is rational, assertive, and competitive, yet men get emotional during momentous events such as the birth of their children or a World Cup final. Yin and Yang constantly transform into each other, eventually winter turns to spring, soon day gives way to night; one without the other results in dis-ease.

Jung described a neurotic person as one who is one-sided, a person who overemphasises one side of her personality to avoid dealing with the other. Well then, our culture is extremely neurotic. Domination, aggression, force and control are at the heart of how our overly masculine world operates. Because feminine qualities such as compassion, empathy, co-operation, nurturing and healing have been discredited and demoted, the world is characterised by abuse of those with lesser power – nations, women, children, nature. People are murdered for frivolous things like cars and cellphones. Women, the elderly and children are raped and abused daily by males, and in some cases, by females as well. We are on the brink of an epic environmental disaster because humans have stripped the environment, wildlife and natural resources. The banking system is collapsing. The gap between the rich and the poor continues to widen, leading to uprisings and "terror" attacks as the oppressed react to continued losses for the benefit of an elite, powerful few. All these are the ills of unmitigated masculinity. When a person, system, culture or society has too little feminine energy and too much masculine energy it places lower value on others than on self – leading to greed, selfishness, aggression, domination and control, the hallmarks of our current culture.

Certain mystics and keepers of history state that before our current patriarchy, the world was predominantly matriarchal. Evidently, men and masculinity were treated as shoddily as women and femininity are treated in the present patriarchy. The world didn't work then either because what is required is not the dominance of one energy over the other, but balanced expression. Unfortunately, it seems the pendulum needed to swing both ways – the oppressed becoming the oppressor – before balance can be restored.

This is a man's world. Look at our vocabulary. Words such as mankind, history, guys are taken to represent everyone. The male pronoun is the standard for denoting people, and God. Our major religions are predominantly about a single (mostly absent) parent,

Father God who art in heaven, which makes me wonder about the glut of earthly fathers who are absent in their children's lives. As above, so below. Most of our religious mythology from Adam and Eve to Prometheus and Pandora carry a clear message that the feminine is manipulative, conniving, duplicitous, untrustworthy and dangerous. Men are the heirs to the throne, the good sons of Father God; women, dodgy non-men, children of a lesser god. The message has been loud and clear: femininity is to be kept in check, and it has been. Only a limited range of feminine attributes are sanctioned, with feminine roles being confined to little more than sex, child bearing, child rearing and care giving. This is an uncomfortably narrow job description. It is no wonder that women have ditched their femininity in droves.

Many women have suppressed their femininity, for survival. We don't want to feel unsafe and vulnerable. We don't want to be seen as weak. We don't want to become victims. For good reason – our world is physically, emotionally, psychologically and sexually abusive to women. So we have put a layer of masculine steel around our soft feminine core. We reserve our femininity for safe spaces, and publicly we express femininity in ways that have received patriarchal approval – which is really only nurturing mother and pliable girl. Elderly women are practically invisible in our society. Females in their childbearing years who choose not to be mothers are disapproved of and viewed with suspicion. This is the life cycle – girlhood, motherhood, invisibility. Patriarchal warmth cools as a woman ages. We understand and comply by attempting to arrest our development; we shave our pubic hair, wage war against the "seven signs of ageing", starve our womanly curves, prop up our maturing boobs, and dye our grey hairs – the same grey hairs that make ageing men look distinguished and wise. These are some of the distractions that keep us from owning our power as women. We are preoccupied with the size of our waistline, the men we have or wish we had, and of course competing with other women for the affection, approval and care of men. Women suffer from Stockholm syndrome. Since being a man is vastly more favoured than being a woman, having the favour of men is more valued than having the favour of women. As Patricia Lynn Reilly observed, "Competition among women is woven into the fabric of a society that prefers men. We compete with each other for the attention of men. Surrounded by images, stories, and attitudes that foster rivalry and suspicion among women, we lose touch with our original connection with the women in our lives."

Compare the personal and professional gossip, judgement and drama-riddled relationships of women with the easy-going, stable, supportive relationships men maintain. Although it makes sense why many women choose masculinity to survive and thrive, we could not have turned against femininity without turning on each other.

Look at the relationship we have with our menstruation, the period pains we suffer and how we generally wage war against those few millilitres of menstrual blood we shed. Phrases such as "having the curse" are commonly used to describe our periods. Our negative attitude towards menstruation poisons how we perceive womanhood, or does is reflect how we perceive womanhood? The onset of your period is the single most significant biological indicator of a girl's transition to womanhood, thus the two are incontrovertibly connected. The sanitary wear industry is designed to help us pretend our period does not exist; the more absorbent and less detectable the product, the better. Then there are the ads of forlorn young women transported by these super-absorbent magic carpets to sandy beaches where they can frolic in the surf in tiny white bikinis, knowing that their cursed menstrual blood has been contained, which for some inexplicable reason is always depicted as a blue liquid. Ironically, one of the worst things you can do for your menstrual cramps is immerse yourself in cold water. The language used in the adverts is dominated by words like freedom, secret, sanitary and protection. Sanitary implies that menstruation is dirty. Protection – what are they protecting us from? What is it that you are being freed from? Tampon is French for "plug" or "bung", a variant from the Old French *tapon* meaning a "piece of cloth to plug a hole", charming isn't it? In fact, have you ever noticed how many products are out there for the shaving, waxing, powdering, cleansing, deodorising, douching and general sanitising of various parts of a woman's body?

I wonder if the fact that we perceive our period as a pain contributes to it often being accompanied by actual physical pain. After all, the monthly period is a woman's reminder of her essential femininity. Louise Hay, author of *You Can Heal Your Life*[32] says, "The probable cause of PMS is allowing for too much confusion, giving your power away to outside influences and rejecting the feminine processes." She suggests the following affirmation to change the mental process that created the issue, "I now take charge of my mind and my life. I am a powerful and dynamic woman! Every part of my body functions perfectly. I love me." This is an acceptance instead of a rejection of your self, period, femininity, creativity and womanhood; a reclamation of your power.

Women have had to exaggerate their masculinity in order to thrive. In the working world, especially, women who make the biggest strides are the ones who can downplay their femininity and become "one of the boys". For years, this was one of my most prized compliments, being seen as one of the boys. Since women generally have to work twice as hard to be deemed half as good as men, we have learned to be even better men than many males! The activist Gloria Steinem famously observed that, "We are becoming the men we wanted to marry." The world is now filled with men, in male and female bodies. It seems women took to heart the adage, "If you can't beat them, join them". We want to talk like men, act like men, think like men, date like men, drive like men, drink like men, deal like men, mate like me. We recently turned entertainer Steve Harvey's book, entitled *Act Like a Lady, Think Like a Man*, into a bestseller and blockbuster movie. How many guys do you think would have mobbed bookshops and cinemas for "Act Like a Gentleman, Think Like a Woman"?

Femininity is in desperate need of good PR. There are many feminine traits that are currently valued in our society which people do not even recognise as feminine. For instance, creativity is greatly reliant on feminine energy, as is long-term vision. To be innovative, you need to connect to the feminine, the unknown. The ability to inspire, to motivate and to influence – these are feminine traits. The feminine evokes, it brings forth, it is the energy of the muse. The feminine is the part of us that values connection and communication, networking, listening, sharing. Emotions, which patriarchy fears because of their unpredictability, are a feminine charge. When you disconnect from the heart – emotions – and rely solely on the mind, you become cold, domineering and controlling; a recipe for wars, greed, exploitation and abuse. Feminine energy is integral to spiritual health, because it is through feelings, intuition and emotions that Spirit speaks to us. You just need to look around to witness the poisonous fruits our culture is reaping through the repression of femininity.

The entire world is affected by this masculine-feminine imbalance, but women suffer more because, naturally, we are meant to carry more feminine energy than men. There are exceptions; women with an innate masculine essence, but they are a minority. If you've managed to get this far in goddess bootcamp, you can safely assume that your essence is feminine. If you would pick love over respect – not that you should ever have to – you have a feminine essence. If the concept of fullness appeals to you more than emptiness, you have a feminine essence. If you prefer to be appreciated for being as opposed to doing, you have a feminine essence.

Leading with our masculine side, as we do now, is akin to going through life with one hand, the dominant hand, tied behind your back – it makes everything that much more difficult and inefficient. As a woman, when you spend the majority of your time functioning from your masculine, you become less effective and more stressed than if you were leading with your feminine. For example, men are physically stronger than women and thus if a hole needed to be dug, a man would do it quicker and suffer less physical stress in the process than if a woman were to do it. Plus his sense of satisfaction from the task would be greater than any woman's. Most women dig metaphoric holes on a daily basis, granted, not always by choice. Women in the workplace complain about feeling stressed and run down far more than their male counterparts because, in most work environments, we lead with our masculine side; easy for men, taxing for women.

Finding the appropriate balance between your own masculine and feminine energy as a woman allows you to create a healthier, more effortless life. As a woman, it is easier to do life in a feminine way. Trust me, this has been a hard pill for me to swallow. I was raised to do things as well as, if not better than, men. I can out-man the average guy without breaking a sweat. I used to enjoy telling guys that I had my own six-pack to stroke since they couldn't seem to manage a couple of sit-ups. Until a few years ago, I didn't even know how to apply make-up. One day I had an epiphany while doing my monthly grocery shopping. The mall was teeming with helpful men, willing to not only direct but escort me to the correct aisle, explain the merits of different brands of Atchaar, of all things, and provide detailed advice on appropriate paints for my amateur arts and crafts project. This was my regular mall, and the guys had never been that helpful, cheerful, witty and attentive. I realised quickly enough that it had everything to do with how I looked. I was wearing tight jeans and a particular pair of wedges that make me wiggle when I walk. Most other patrons were in their usual month-end, Saturday morning grocery shopping uniform; mismatched tracksuits, mommy jeans, oversized T-shirts, flip-flops, and a good dose of bed hair. That is usually how I would have looked too, if it hadn't been for a morning meeting. I am an attractive woman. I say that without a hint of arrogance. I am merely stating a fact. I was brought up to revere intellect, self-sufficiency and achievement. For most of my life I have been mildly annoyed by my physical attractiveness and often went out of my way to downplay it. My inclination is towards muted colours, a bare face and a fuss-free hairstyle – basically a step short of wearing a sign saying, "engage only with my brain". Some years ago I realised that this behaviour was limiting and decided to balance my childhood conditioning by wearing more colour, skirts and dresses, make-up and accessories. It was a form of DIY therapy; not very successful, I might add, because inside I still wanted to be noticed only for my brain (masculine) and not beauty (feminine). That day, while I was shopping for groceries in high heels, I finally got it. Being attractive – a feminine attribute – is fun and powerful. I had complete strangers wanting to please me, because it pleased them to please me. It gave me access to a source of power, inspiration and motivation that, until then, I had hardly ever used and it was fun and effortless. Men are great at digging holes, women rock at getting men to love digging holes for us.

Fun.

Effortlessness.

Ease.

The way of a goddess.

As a woman with a feminine essence, you cannot have full access to your power without embracing your femininity. Feminine power is different from masculine power, but it is certainly not inferior. While masculine power is assertive – it is an active, doing energy; feminine power is attractive – it is a receptive, being energy. Evelet, imagine how much more fulfilling your life would be if you harnessed the power to attract the things you want, instead of always having to go club them on the head and drag them home yourself. I think all exhausted women – and there are plenty of us – could use a good dose of attractive feminine power.

In restoring femininity to its rightful place, we help temper rampant, out of balance masculinity in ourselves and our men. It is an opportunity to restore health all round. Subconsciously, men exhibit self-hate and mistrust at the present day expression of masculinity. They freak out when their daughters reach dating age, and they lose respect for a woman after they have slept with her. Like Groucho Marx, they do not want to become a member of any club that will have them. Healthy masculine energy, on the other hand, is a thing of beauty. It is the energy of the leader: radiant, strong, rational, decisive, confident, assertive, active, focused, giving and warm. Feminine energy is just as powerful. It is soft, receptive, inclusive, non-judgemental, inspirational, colourful, unlimited, heart-based, refreshing and expansive. If feminine energy is a flowing river, masculine energy provides the banks that contain it. If masculine energy is the outlines of a drawing, feminine energy provides the colours that transform the lines and shapes into a vibrant piece of art, pulsing with life. This is the ultimate power couple. We owe it to ourselves, and the world, to give feminine power room to flourish.

Becoming A Goddess: Being Feminine and Powerful

112. Where is your comfort zone? Take a piece of paper and, on one side, write all the attributes and beliefs you associate with masculinity. On the other side, write all the attributes and beliefs you associate with femininity. You can also refer to the Yin-Yang diagram. Explore how you feel about these associations and how they affect your behaviour. For instance, if you associate strength with masculinity, how does that affect how you behave? Is the belief that strength is masculine accompanied by another, that femininity is weak? If you believe that women shouldn't have to work, how does that affect how you approach and feel about work? Do you require any adjustments in your beliefs and behaviour to be more resonant with your new choice of an effortless life of ease?

113. Build your feminine muscle. Whenever you are in a position where you can occupy the feminine space, do. Allow a man, or another woman occupying a masculine space, to lead, guide, decide, protect or provide while you nurture, nourish, motivate, inspire, influence and support. Start with the small things, like dinner plans and household chores.

114. Get the man out of the boy. Sexual attraction requires polarity; opposite poles, like the negative and positive ends of magnets. Very feminine women attract very masculine men. While women with little feminine energy attract men with little masculine energy and you find yourself saddled

with masculine responsibilities. A lot of women complain that their men are not carrying their weight so they have to do everything themselves. This is a catch-22 situation. The more you do, the more you have to do, leading to a spiral of stress, exhaustion and resentment. I used to expect men to out-man me, but the only way to attract a masculine man – if that's what you want – is to become a feminine woman. If you stop being the man, he will start or leave.

115. Flirt. This is a quick and easy way to get into a feminine space. Flirt with babies, puppies, construction workers, telesales people, and bald geriatrics.

116. Seek a feminine role model. There are always women who wield their feminine power with grace; women who seem to achieve their goals in a soft, firm yet gentle manner; who appear to have a lot done for them – that is, with a great ability to attract, motivate, inspire and influence. Find one to emulate. Pay attention to how she behaves and relates.

117. Get acquainted with your inner woman and inner man. Take some time to yourself, with your journal close at hand. Imagine that you are sitting in a theatre, by yourself, and call your inner male on to the stage. Look at his appearance. Is he tall or short, muscular or scrawny? How is he dressed? Have a conversation with him. Get to know him like you would an external person. What are his likes and dislikes, fears, dreams. You can even ask his opinion on aspects of your life or challenges. Write down all the impressions you received. Repeat the exercise with your inner female. Visit with your inner male and female occasionally and eventually, when it feels right, introduce them to each other. You want your masculine and feminine side to work as a team. As within, so without. Once they work well together, you will work well with the men in your external world.

118. Learn to reside in a feminine space.
    a. Occupy your body. One of the quickest ways to shift from a mental, masculine space into a feminine space is to move into your body and heart. Take up an activity, such as dancing or some forms of yoga, which increases your awareness of your body. The more you occupy and are aware of your body the easier it will be for you to activate your feminine power.
    b. The third-eye (Aina), heart (Anahata), and sacral/womb (Svadhisthana) chakras are feminine chakras. Learn to shift your consciousness into your heart and your womb space. As you talk to people, become aware of your heart space. An easy way to do this is by imagining that you are breathing in and out through your heart. Refer to session 7: Free Your Heart. You move your awareness into your womb the same way you move it into your heart. By deliberately becoming aware of it, you can even flex your vaginal muscles to help you locate your womb area. Whenever you want to activate or amp up your feminine energy, move your consciousness into your womb.

119. Celebrate Friday the 13th. Friday the 13th is not unlucky; in fact it is packed with juicy feminine power. Friday is named after a woman, Freyja the Nordic goddess of fertility, celebration and passion. Long before we used the current Grecian calendar, the calendar was based on the moon, which orbits the earth 13 times a year. The moon is one of two planets associated with women – the other is Venus – making 13 a feminine number. The moon has a direct influence on women's menstrual cycle. When women are not exposed to artificial lighting and hormones (e.g., the pill) their cycle synchronises with the moon. If there was ever a day designed to host the celebration of femininity it is Friday the 13th. We usually get about three of these a year. Next time, use it to host a celebration of the feminine.

120. Divine Intervention: I'll have to go with Freyja as a good goddess to help you enjoy your femininity and Lilith to remind you that you can be feminine and powerful.

I play for all teams; there are more than two.
I cheer for the Virgin Mary, and I root for Jezebel
Notice the Scarlett letter stitched on my habit
I AM strengthened by my weaknesses
I AM a superhero on chronic meds
I carry darkness within my light
I AM humbled by my arrogance
I like to look saintly while I sin
My lies plant seeds of truth
I blow hot when I AM cold
I AM a horny angel
I AM a friendly foe
I AM everything
Full of myself
I AM becoming whole

"Remembering Myself", by Kagiso Msimango

Remember Yourself

The thing that is really hard, and really amazing, is giving up on being perfect and beginning the work of becoming yourself.

~ Anna Quindlen

Evie, are you full of yourself?

Imagine that at birth you were like a huge mansion with numerous rooms, each room representing an aspect of your unique being. In the beginning you freely expressed all aspects of yourself. The doors and windows to the rooms of your mansion were wide open. However, soon you began to realise that not all your facets were accepted. You were educated explicitly that certain expressions are unacceptable – "Nobody loves a smarty pants!" – and implicitly, such as when your mother slapped the back of your head for asking that really fat lady if she eats too much. In response, you began to close certain rooms in your mansion. You learned to open others in particular circumstances only, for instance only touching your genitals in private, or only sounding intelligent when boys weren't around. Certain rooms, you boarded up permanently. I know men who haven't shed a tear since primary school and women who won't masturbate. As you go through life, you draw up the curtains here, close windows there, shut a door or two and even wall up some rooms like they never existed. By adulthood, many of us, despite owning the Taj Mahal, occupy the space of a Formula 1 hotel room. Because we have disconnected from so many aspects of our being, we experience a sense of lack, which we tend to diagnose as not-enoughness; not good enough, clever enough, popular enough, pretty enough, funny enough, talented enough... the list goes on. We are bewildered by the futility of our attempts to appease our not-enoughness by feeding it things, because we can only restore our wholeness by allowing more out, not getting more in.

How would your life be different if you were whole, Evie? Mine became literally more colourful as I reclaimed a particular part of myself. When I was young, I hero worshipped my uncle, Tshepo. With great difficulty, I drank raw eggs because he drank raw eggs. I went fishing and camping because he did. Whatever I could do to emulate or impress him, I did. For some reason *Malome* Tshepo had a thing against make-up and nail polish. He would disdainfully describe make-up as "wearing a disguise" and complained how some women went up in a puff of multi-coloured dust when you so much as sat next to them. I felt that decorating myself was wrong, even though I did not know why. I would apply nail polish when I was away at boarding school, feeling guilty and disobedient the way other kids do when sneaking a cigarette, but I never wore make-up. Along the way, I realised that not all the issues I carried were mine and started detangling myself from some inherited issues. I'd apply make-up for very special occasions, but I sucked at it. Since I did not experiment with cosmetics in my teens and twenties, anything more complicated than applying eye-liner, mascara and lip gloss was beyond me. I sheepishly asked a friend of mine, Lulu, who manages communications for a cosmetics house, to give me lessons. What she did instead was arrange for me to get lessons from a professional make-up artist. There was a catch. The session would be at the cosmetics counter of the very big clothing store at Melrose Arch (read, in public) and I would have to tweet and blog about it. I was hoping for clandestine lessons at her house. Talk about having to face your issues head on! I had to confront a lot of fear and shame in that short period, but when I left that store after the session I felt like I had dropped 10 kilos of psychological baggage.

None of us are born disapproving of ourselves, Evie. It is something we are taught. Nobody has the authority to tell you which parts of you are right and which are wrong, but they do. Many people, especially parents and caregivers, do so with good intentions; they want you to fit in and be accepted by society. However, as soon as you are old enough to be discerning, you have a responsibility to yourself to review those judgements. You must restore yourself to wholeness. For instance, you may still decide that it is inappropriate to fiddle with your clitoris at the dinner table, but you should free yourself of the sexual shame; you are neither bad nor dirty for deriving sexual pleasure from your own organs.

A life of WOWness does not require you to be perfect, but you do need to be whole. It is vital that you retrieve, accept, embrace and heal your disowned parts. Because of the way the universe functions, the qualities that you suppress and reject in yourself will have to be confronted though the mirror of relationships.

For years I was a magnet for inconsiderate, self-serving people; lovers, friends, relatives and colleagues. These users were attracted to me like a moth to a user-friendly flame because I was absolutely terrified of being seen as selfish. I'd bend over backwards to fulfil the needs of others. It started when I was a schoolgirl. At home they used to cook big Sunday lunches, so there'd be food left over for supper. One pre-microwave Sunday, feeling a bit peckish after lunch, I put the roast in the oven to reheat and promptly forgot about it. I left to visit a friend. My aunt came home to a smoke-filled kitchen and a smouldering pile of ashes where the roast had been. When I returned hours later, she descended on me like a deranged Banshee, accusing me of greedily stuffing my face and then selfishly burning the rest of the food. She was clearly having a bad day, but as irrational as her accusation was, it became etched on my psyche, making me terrified of being viewed as selfish. For years I catered for and even anticipated the demands of all and sundry, in the quest of avoiding that dreaded label. I became a popular hive for user bees. Eventually in my late twenties, out of sheer exhaustion, I violently tore down the door to my selfishness room and rescued my selfish bitch self. When the users came as usual; demanding chicks with gaping mouths, chanting; "me, me, me", I responded, "me too!" They were angry, confused and, of course, repelled. The number of people in my life dwindled rapidly, but I was free and happy. Now sometimes I am selfless and sometimes I am selfish, but I get to choose.

Allow me to retell, from a different perspective, the tale of the little soul, which I related during session 10 – this time to illustrate how misguided our habitual rejection of self is. In the beginning Spirit/God/Source was all there is. There was nothing else. Because It was *all there is*, It could know Itself but could not experience Itself. In the absence of *that which is not, that which is* cannot experience itself. Spirit knew what It was, but without anything to compare Itself with there was no way of experiencing who It was. Experience of self requires an other. Like the cheeky bumper sticker that says, "Will you go away if I promise to miss you?" you cannot long for someone's presence unless they are absent. You wouldn't know hot from cold if you had only ever experienced one constant temperature. So Spirit needed something against which to experience Itself. But because It was *all there is* the only way it could experience Itself was by becoming more than one, by separating into seemingly separate souls. These souls would be able to experience themselves in relation to each other. They are us. We can experience ourselves in relation to each other and, through us, Spirit can experience Itself. Spirit created the universe because it wanted to experience itself.

Evie, you are Spirit incarnate. You truly are a goddess. There is no reason to reshape your true self because you originate from divinity. You have an exquisite reason to exist, fulfilling Spirit's desire to experience Itself; all aspects of Itself, even those that we may deem as bad, shameful or unacceptable. They are all part of this divine plan of Spirit to experience Itself. When other people anger, confuse and even disgust you – as they are inclined to do – remember that they, too, are a spark of the Divine. Not only that, but in experiencing yourself through them you get to know who you are. They are a gift to you. Attempting to be a one-dimensional, all good, perfect shiny Evie sabotages your divine purpose.

Daughter of Eve, your duty is not to be perfect, it is to be you, all of you. Even as you choose not to express certain aspects of your being, release them without judgement. Don't suppress them because you deem them bad or unacceptable. Be bad, be good, be free, be whole, be true, be you.

It's hard to express yourself as a whole, multi-coloured and multi-faceted being. Part of our legacy, as daughters of Eve, is carrying the shame of our progenitor. When Eve wanted to occupy a bigger space, and she crossed the line within which she was supposed to be happily confined, she doomed humanity for all eternity; or so the story goes. This Scarlet letter tattooed on the walls of our very cells inclines us to prefer crouching in smallness over standing in fullness. It helps to remember that Eve is not the genesis of our history; before Eve there was Lilith.

According to early Hebraic Creation myth, Lilith was Adam's first wife. Yes, that Adam. She was created independently from and equal to Adam. God made both of them from the Earth, which made them equals. Like many partnerships of equals there were disagreements and power struggles between Adam and Lilith. In an attempt to assert himself over his partner, Adam insisted that Lilith always lay beneath him – in the missionary position – during lovemaking. Right then an angel should've descended from heaven and smacked Adam on the head with a copy of *Cosmopolitan*. As expected, this ridiculous demand led to a particularly heated argument, which Lilith ended by uttering the name of God – an ancient equivalent of saying "kiss my arse" – and storming off.

When Adam realised that Lilith was not coming back, he went to God whining about being abandoned and pleaded with God to get Lilith back. God sent three angels, called Senoy, Sansenoy, and Semangelof, to find Lilith and persuade her to go back home. They found her, but it did not go too well; you know what they say about when a woman's fed up. Not only did they fail to sweet-talk her into going back, but they ended up banishing her to the Outer Darkness (this is a long story, I am paraphrasing it here).

Lilith was then replaced with Eve. Unlike Lilith, Eve was not created as an equal from the Earth, but from Adam's rib. She was an external manifestation of Adam's inner woman. Eve was Adam's concept of what a woman should be. Even though Lilith was banished to the underworld she would occasionally sneak back to the Garden of Eden, where Adam now lived with Eve. You know that drive-by past the ex's house that you need to get out of your system on your road to recovery. When she saw Eve, she lamented the fate of her fellow sister, who was basically a biblical cross between a Stepford wife and a blow-up doll. Remember, she was made how Adam felt a woman should be, and Adam doesn't sound like he had much depth. I can't help but judge him for that missionary position stunt. Lilith decided to rescue Eve. She appeared before Eve as a serpent, which in ancient times was a symbol of healing, and encouraged Eve to eat the fruit of knowledge, giving her an opportunity to become her own person. Eve took the offer, sunk her teeth into that forbidden fruit and saw the light. The rest, as they say in the classics, is history.

Before Eve, there was Lilith. The mansion came before the shack. There is more to you, Evelet. Remember. To remember has two meanings, both equally important on our path to WOWness. To remember is to have something come to mind again, to remember what has been forgotten. To re-member is also to put something back together again, you remember what has been dismembered. Evelet, remember all your hidden and rejected aspects, and restore yourself back to wholeness. Embrace them all. The time has come to bid sweet adieu to Evelet, daughter of Eve, made of Adam's rib. We are due for a big, audacious bite out of that juicy forbidden fruit. As Laurel Thatcher Ulrich rightly pointed out by making it the title of her book, "Well-behaved women rarely make history."

What is the point of working so hard for goddesshood if you are not going to shake up the world just a little – or a lot?

Goodbye Evelet, hello Lily.

Becoming A Goddess: Re-membering Yourself

120. Re-member yourself. Recall who you were before you disowned parts of yourself. If you cannot recall, imagine. Ask yourself, how might I have been before I was so small? Rejoin with your disowned aspects. Refer to the actions in session 5.

121. How would your life be different if you gave yourself permission to be whole, Lily? What kind of life would you lead if you loved yourself completely, and showed all your colours as you did at the very beginning? What would you stop chasing? What would you allow to catch you? Write a list of things you would start doing, stop doing, do differently. Pick three that intimidate you the least and implement them. Wait for God to smite you or your world to collapse. If neither of these calamitous events comes to pass, implement the rest of the list, one "fuck you" at a time.

122. Practice unconditional love and acceptance. Refer to session 16 on learning to accept yourself as you are.

123. Throw a coming-out party. Host a party where everyone can come as a disowned persona. If you've disapproved of loud, attention-seeking people, dress in an outrageous, brightly coloured outfit, monopolise conversations, talk and laugh too loud. Be that person you have always judged. Serve lots of forbidden foods. Remember to invite me.

124. Divine Intervention: Of course we want to invite Lilith to this party. The ass-kicking Hindu goddess Durga and passionate Pele are others you want on your team as you reclaim your disowned parts.

Own Your Sexy

Does my sexiness upset you?
Does it come as a surprise that I dance like I've got
diamonds at the meeting of my thighs?
~ Maya Angelou
"Still I Rise"

How do you feel about your sexiness, Lily?

Boy am I glad you are finally here, Lily. This is not a session Evelet would have coped with. But I know you are a big, whole girl, so I am going to jump straight into it. What do you call your genitals?

This session is really a continuation of the previous one, however re-membering your genitals is so important on our path to WOWness that it deserved its own bootcamp session. It is important that we get into your pants, Lily, for a number of reasons. Your relationship with your genitals affects (1) your relationship with yourself as a woman, which in turns affects all your other relationships, (2) the amount of pleasure in your life, all aspects of your life, not just sexual, and (3) your personal power. There are actually many more reasons, which could fill an entire book, but for our purposes we will focus on just these three.

Let's start with the obvious, as Miss B figured out at the tender age of three when she asked me, "Mommy how did you know that I am a girl?" and promptly answered herself, "Is it because I have a nunu?" Yes, Lily, you are a girl because you have a nunu, despite what the IAAF tried to pull on super-athlete Caster Semenya.

Your gender is a big part of your identity and how you experience life, and your genitals are a big part of your gender. I often ask this question, "What do you call your genitals?" at The Goddess Academy playshops and gatherings because it is hard to have a relationship with something you don't have a name for. After a shocked, uncomfortable silence, most respond with the word vagina, which I reject because it's usually a cop-out. If you also said vagina, Lily, let me ask you this: excluding any visits to a doctor, how many times in the past two months have you even said the word vagina?

Usually, after a bit of prodding, I get some real answers to this question. Sadly, but not surprisingly, most of the responses start with, "My boyfriend/husband calls it..." So let me clarify: I am interested in what you call your genitals. They are your genitals, should you not have a name for them?

I have four names for mine. It's not because I am an overachiever, it demonstrates how much our society has managed to alienate sexuality when you need four names to refer to one thing. Most of my other body parts manage with only one name each. My nose is always my nose in all contexts. It has coped pretty well without pseudonyms. Why is it that our buttocks, breasts and genitals have to have aliases and multiple personalities, but our livers and shins don't? Heed the sagacious words of DH Lawrence, "The word arse is as much God as the word face. It must be so, otherwise you cut off your God at the waist." Anyway, I digress. My genitals go by four names. For gynaecological visits I take my vagina, which is only ever seen by medical personnel, who mainly want to prod it with cold, stainless-steel instruments. I also have a nunu, which came into regular use with the arrival of Miss B, a big fan of nunus. Nunus are a big part of our lives, Miss B and I. We talk about them, maintain their cleanliness, check them for rashes, we part them with our fingers and inspect them in the mirror. Recently, Miss B asked me to check her four-year-old nunu for pubic hair; alas it had none. So I have a vagina for people who expect to get paid to touch it and a nunu, which never costs me money, is my non-medical, non-sexual, communal vagina. For sexual purposes I have a pussy and a yoni. Which one I use depends on my attitude to my sexuality and sexual activity at the given time. Yoni is a beautiful *Sanskrit* word, used in Tantra to refer to female sexual organs. There are various translations of the word, all equally reverent, "source/origin of life", "divine passage" or "sacred space". My yoni only shows up when there is a strong spiritual element to my sexual activities. For more casual and mundane sexual interactions I have a pussy. The word makes me think of cats, which I happen to like. They are sensual, slinky, content, self-possessed and beautiful. When you see a cat you want to stroke it and the best part is that they enjoy being stroked, they are gracious receivers. Cats only do what gives them pleasure, and they have very high opinions of themselves. I also like the fact that many of the sexy ancient goddesses are associated with felines. Bast, the Egyptian goddess of sensual pleasure, is also known as the cat goddess and was believed to transform into a cat at night. Sekhmet, another Egyptian goddess, is connected with lions and was often depicted with a lion's head and a woman's body. During the reign of Bast and Sekhmet the cat became the symbol of goddess energy. Freyja, the Norse goddess of passion, rode in a chariot pulled by two mighty cats. These are the reason why I refer to my genitals as pussy. But enough about my pussy. We are here to discuss yours. Lily, it is important that you acknowledge your pussy, connect with it and establish a relationship with it. A great way to start is by naming it.

The name I like the least in my quartet is vagina. Firstly, it is inaccurate. Vagina is the name of only one part, the passage between the vulva and the uterus, in what is really a system of organs. Women have a range of sexual organs, more of a sexual system really. Besides the vagina, there's the labia majora, labia minora, the mons veneris, the perineum, the clitoris, and more. Secondly, the meaning of the word vagina is "sheath for a sword". We can safely assume that in this case the sword refers to a penis. Sword sheath does not evoke happy, warm or juicy feelings in me, I don't know about you Lily. In fact it fits perfectly with the cold stainless-steel instruments the gynaecologist uses to separate me with my cash. I especially dislike the implication that the vagina's primary role is to cover the sword, making me suspect that it was named by men, (and honestly, I don't want any man who thinks of his penis as a sword anywhere near my nunu, pussy or yoni)! Sadly, many women seem to behave like it really is primarily a sheath for a penis. They seem unaware that you don't need a single penis to unleash the power and pleasure of the pussy.

I know a young woman – let's call her Khanyi – who gained the favour of the gods and had a Ferrari bestowed upon her. They felt that she deserved something utterly precious, lovingly crafted and exquisitely magnificent; a limitless source of pleasure, power and perhaps even a few miracles. Khanyi seldom drives the Ferrari, and she can drive. In fact, if she didn't need to take it to the car wash or service she would easily go for months without driving it. Like most mortals, she enjoys herself thoroughly when she gets behind the wheel of this sexy beast. In fact, there are very few things in her life that compare to the pleasure of letting that powerful engine loose on the open road. Alas, Khanyi is constantly plagued with guilt and shame when she drives her car. So she mostly just rides in it while someone else, usually a man, does the driving. Most men consider it a punishable offence to leave a Ferrari gathering dust in the garage so they try their luck and ask to drive it. Depending on some personal criteria, Khanyi turns some men down and presents the keys to others. Unfortunately, many of the guys who've had access to this precious work of technical and aesthetic art cannot tell Enzo Ferrari from Vuyo Mbuli. This is usually because often, when Khanyi relinquishes the keys, she is really dying for a spin in that fine car, and any old driver will do. As if this wasn't weird enough, when she is with other Ferrari owners – they hang out – she often lies about driving the car. She fibs about not driving the car too and, at times, even about whom she allows to drive the car and why. Yep, Khanyi has a very unfortunate relationship with her precious possession. However twisted Khanyi's relationship with her divine gift may be, it is not unusual. Many women treat their pussies the way Khanyi treats her Ferrari. Like we are merely babysitting them for a lover; we are just the carriers, the sheath for the sword. Betty Dodson, the renowned sex educator, remarked with irritation, "The characters in *Sex and the City* were all scrambling for a man. I don't call that a good message for women. Couldn't just one of them say, 'Look, I prefer to masturbate than go out with another one of these jerks'?"

Lily, if you agree that your pussy is an inextricable part of your being, identity, gender, femininity and power, then you surely must realise that you cannot fully accept and re-member yourself or harness your feminine power until you have owned it.

Your relationship with your pussy affects your capacity for pleasure. For starters, the clitoris is the only human organ whose sole function is to give pleasure. God(dess) bestowed it upon us, women. Take a moment to let that sink in. Women own the only organ whose sole purpose is to give pleasure to its owner – and mostly we do nothing with it.

Lily, if you were the financial director of an organisation, would you give more money to a manager who never spends her budget? Yet we expect our partners, life, and spirit, to increase the bliss in our lives when we hardly exploit the pleasure that is already ours to have. As within, so without. Your outer world is always a reflection of your inner world. You cannot expect the world to treat you like a fabulous goddess, and lay juicy gifts at your feet when you have such a tenuous relationship with the very part of yourself that makes you a woman and gives you free and easy access to sheer bliss. Lily, you need to make a commitment to re-member your pussy.

After introductions, start exploring your pussy. Get to know how it looks and feels. *Glamour* magazine recently validated information that I have known for a long time – because I have asked – that 84 per cent of men believe they can pick their penis from a line up. And you know what Lily? I bet it's not really an issue for the 16 per cent who can't because they can always call out to them. Men are famous for naming their penises. Most women wouldn't know their genitals from a bucket of oysters.

Yes, men's sexual organs are on the outside of their bodies, making them pretty hard to ignore. Men also have a relatively healthier relationship with sex than women do. Society does not sexually repress men to the same degree, and in the same ways, as it does women. Men do not suffer as many mixed messages as women do; with women when you love sex "too much" you are a nymphomaniac and if you don't love it enough you are frigid. You have sex "too quickly and easily" you are a slut; you don't you are a tease. I get all of this and acknowledge the shame, mixed messages, fears, guilt and pain associated with female genitalia and sexuality. However I still insist that you go there. Luckily I am asking you to put your pussy in the hands, literally, of someone you can trust – you.

The sky is not going to fall on your head if you masturbate, and you will not grow hair on your palms either, despite what you've been told. When Miss B got a new nanny, who was not yet initiated in our nunu-loving ways she admonished Miss B for touching her nunu. She told my nunu-loving girl child to, "Never, ever do that again. We never touch the nunu!" she declared. I asked her why we never touch the nunu and she looked at me like I was brain damaged. I persisted: was it bad for Miss B's health, the health of others in her vicinity, detrimental to her soul perhaps, or maybe the environment? Typically, she only touches her own nunu for issues of hygiene, if not to provide access to a man. I asked her to go and think about why this must be so and, when she came back, she admitted that she could not think of a single good reason, other than her upbringing. As you examine your relationship with your genitals and sexuality, Lily, remember the words of the Indian mystic Osho, "Your whole idea about yourself is borrowed, borrowed from those who have no idea who they are themselves." I encourage you to take your sexual pleasure into your own hands, eagerly, regularly, and reverently.

Here is a nice party trick you can use to swiftly end a conversation with your girlfriends. Announce, eagerly, "I can't wait to get home. I am going to take a nice, long candle-lit bubble bath and then I am going to find out how many different kinds of orgasms I can give myself." Some women will forgive you if you are single, sexually frustrated or both, but if you are happily coupled and sexed-up, admitting to self-pleasuring to women (most men love it) elicits the same reaction as drowning kittens. Many women mistakenly believe that sex is something you are only supposed to do it with someone else. In this case men know better. We think that self-pleasure is a poor substitute for sex with another, much like we feel that self-love is something you cultivate only if you can't find someone else to love you. Actually, as I have said numerous times in bootcamp, your relationship with yourself sets the tone for all your relationships with others.

Women in our society generally do not find sex as enjoyable as men do. By and large we want sex less often than our male partners. It has been frequently reported that many women would pick a good slab of chocolate over sex. A recent study by *Fitness* magazine in North America asked female readers if they would sacrifice a full year of sex to be skinny. Over 50 per cent said they would. Why wouldn't we go for chocolates and miraculous weight-loss when good sex is so irregular for us? Most men take orgasms as a given, whereas for us it is mostly a hit or miss, and some women have never experienced an orgasm during sexual intercourse. This is because we hardly get any sex education, beyond the biology of it and the little that we glean from the ignoramuses that came before us tends to be extremely male oriented.

Men and women are built differently sexually. For instance women's (yin) sexual energy is diffused throughout the body and, during arousal, it moves from the outside in, whereas men's (yang) sexual energy is focused in the genitals. This is why you can go straight to a man's genitals and he will be aroused, but that is probably the worst approach you can take with a woman. Women take much longer than men to be aroused enough to have orgasmic sex, and we actually take longer than men (and women) think we should. Few people realise that vaginal lubrication is a sign of early arousal. We think it is a "go" when in fact the juices say "get set". However, if you go by Hollywood directors, both porno and mainstream, you'd believe that all that a healthy woman needs to climax is five minutes of good pounding that commences as soon as her vagina is moist enough to accommodate a penis without too much discomfort. This of course couldn't be further from the truth. The owner of a sensuality boutique for women informed me that most of their married clients in their mid-thirties view sex as a chore they need to endure for the sake of their relationship. This is when women are supposed to be reaching their sexual peak. This extract from Devi Ward's *Vagina Monologues*[33] could have been written by any one of millions of women in our society:

Until very recently, my primary relationship with my yoni was one of subtle shame, though if you had asked me at the time, I would have described the feeling as "shy". Shy, and slightly embarrassed, and in absolute fear about communicating verbally to a man about which sensations were pleasurable, and which were not. I would not have described myself as sexually repressed in any way, quite the opposite in fact. I considered myself very sexually open and expressive, and probably was by conventional standards. During the 2–7 minutes of sexual intercourse that is considered "normal" in conventional Western sexuality, I remember experiencing pain in some areas of my yoni and thinking that was natural. I remember that just about the time I started to really FEEL pleasure during sex, the man would ejaculate, and it would be over. I remember having this internal sense of being rushed during oral sex, like I needed to hurry up and come as quickly as I could, because lord knows he won't be down there for long! And gosh, if on the rare occasion he was, I felt embarrassed and uncomfortable, and had a sense of doing him a great disservice by taking so long... just fuck me now ok?

It is unlikely that during the ordinary course of your life, you will come across someone who will be more invested in your sexual pleasure than you are. An erotic angel who will teach you how sex and arousal works for women, hence the preference for chocolate and slim hips over sex. Linda E Savage, a psychologist and sex therapist, reported, "Women seek sex therapy because they fear that there is something terribly wrong with their sexuality. They have lived so long under the shadow of the male model of woman as pleaser that very few have an independent view of their sexual selves." You are unlikely to learn from a man what really pleases you as a woman, but you can learn from your own hand and then teach your men.

Woody Allen looks at masturbation the right way, "Don't knock masturbation, it is sex with someone you love." That is precisely how I would like you to approach it, as an act of self-love. Touch is very important to humans. Touching is one of our first languages of love, and one of the very first senses we develop. While we are still in the womb, as we are caressed by the amniotic fluid, we are cushioned and hugged and massaged by our mother's womb. New-borns fail to thrive and some die when deprived of touch. When you touch someone you communicate tender feelings and intimacy towards them; the opposite is expressed by the refusal to have physical contact with someone. Think about how your recoil from the touch of a stranger, an enemy or someone you are upset with. Based on the amount of touch your genitals receive from you at the moment, do you think your yoni experiences you as friend or stranger? Touch your genitals, so they know you love them. Touch them so you can learn to love them. If you want others to show them love, you must go, and come, first. As within, so without.

In infanthood we literally play with ourselves as we discover each new bit. Our parents think it's cute when we discover our toes and we stare at them, wiggle them and stick them in our mouth, but the minute we find our clitoris and we explore it with the same enthusiasm the reaction is different. Whatever our feelings about it, masturbation is almost always our first sexual activity.

Even in-utero, we touch ourselves for relaxation and pleasure. In 1986, Dr I Meizner captured the first sonographic footage of in-utero masturbation. The *American Journal of Obstetrics and Gynecology*[34] reported, "We recently observed a female fetus at 32 weeks' gestation touching the vulva with the fingers of the right hand. The caressing movements were centred primarily on the region of the clitoris. Movements stopped after 30 to 40 seconds and started again after a few minutes. Furthermore, these slight touches were repeated and were associated with short, rapid movements of pelvis and legs."

Lily, there is absolutely nothing wrong with taking matters into your own hands, it is natural and good for you. (1) You get to practice self-love, through loving touch. (2) Orgasms. (3) Giving yourself pleasure allows you to access more pleasure in other aspects of your life, including when you have sex with a partner. You can help your sexual partners with some show and tell. (4) Orgasms. (5) You build a loving relationship with your femaleness and feminine identity. (6) Orgasms. (7) You start to become familiar with your erotic power, it's nature, as well as how to build it and move it around your body. (8) Orgasms.

In the very first session of bootcamp we spoke about the fact that living is about creating. We are constantly making choices and taking actions that create our lives. A basic definition of creativity is the coming together of known but separate forces to produce a new, previously unknown or unmanifest force. This is how procreation works; two known forces – you through your egg and him through his sperm – come together and produce a new, previously unmanifest force – the baby. Although creativity is not limited to procreation, sexuality and creativity are intertwined. In fact, both creativity and sexuality are governed by the sacral chakra. The other chakra that governs creativity is the throat chakra. The sacral chakra is feminine, and the throat chakra is masculine; once again demonstrating the need for co-operation and co-creation between the masculine and the feminine. The sacral chakra is also in charge of abundance, self-love, self-acceptance, personal power and intuition. The first two chakras, the base chakra and the sacral chakra, are both responsible for sex and sexuality. Yang sexual energy is more concentrated in the base chakra, while yin sexual energy is mostly concentrated in the sacral chakra. So the relationship between sexuality and all the other areas governed by the sacral chakra is stronger in women. As a woman, when you restrict your sexual energy, you block all of these things. The sacral chakra governs your water element, which is what gives your life flow. Water keeps blood pulsing through your physical body and energy moving in your physical and energetic bodies. Your relationship with your sexuality literally affects your life force. The more sexually empowered you are the more intuitive you will be. Intuition allows you to be a primary authority in your own life. It reduces your need to look externally for guidance. With a healthy sexual relationship with yourself, you will have a better relationship with your emotions. You will also be more inclined to have an abundance consciousness (there is enough for everybody) rather than a poverty consciousness, which see resources as limited (there isn't enough time, money, good men) and the self as limited (I am not good enough, attractive enough, clever enough). Does it make sense to you now why a patriarchal society would prefer and cultivate sexually repressed women, Lily?

For oppression to survive, the oppressors must claim, co-opt, distort or corrupt the sources of power available to the oppressed. That is why those in power have HIStorically been interested in our sex lives. Telling us when to have sex, with whom, how and for what reasons, conditioning us that sex is bad, dirty and wrong, and even getting us to believe that – despite all the other things plaguing the country, continent, planet and universe – what God(dess) is really concerned about is what your pussy gets up to. Sexual power is formidable and feminine sexual power that much more so. It is the root of women's innate alchemical ability to take anything and transform it into something of greater value. Innately, women can transform any figurative lead into gold. Lily, think about all the men you've managed to clean up, turning them from duds to studs. It is our kiss (erotic power) that turns the frog into a prince. We are natural alchemists. Look at how you can take one sperm into your womb and ten moons later produce a fully formed infant. You can do the same with your energetic womb, manifesting all your dreams and heart's true desires, but first you need to stop cutting yourself off at the waist and reclaim your pussy power.

Your goddess power is connected to your pussy power.

Becoming a Goddess: Embracing Your Pussy Power

Get to know your pussy.

125. Take a handheld mirror and have a look at all your lady parts. Look at the size, shape, colour and texture of everything on the outside. Feel around on the outside and as far as you can reach on the inside. Be sure you are lubricated before you poke around on the inside.

126. Must Read: Sheri Winston's *Women's Anatomy of Arousal: Secret Maps To Buried Pleasure*. This book will guide you through your sexual organs and how to become a master of your sexual pleasure with or without a partner.

Discover the beauty of your pussy.

127. A lot of women think their labia look ugly; they are too big, uneven, too dark, too bright and so one. How do you know? How many labia have you actually seen to reach this conclusion, especially if you are a heterosexual female? Do not use porn to judge anything, they bleach their labia, glue them into place and even undergo labiaplasty – cosmetic surgery to alter their vulva. You are better off asking the opinion of a heterosexual man or a lesbian about the relative aesthetic appeal of your pussy. Whatever its shape and colours I am certain there is absolutely nothing wrong with your labia. Nunus come in different shapes, sizes and colours. Jamie McCarthy, the artist who built the great wall of vaginas, which is made out of casts of the nunus of 400

women, said, "Vulvas and labia are as different as faces and many people, particularly women, don't seem to know that... For many women their genitals are a source of shame rather than pride and this piece seeks to redress the balance, showing that everyone is different and everyone is normal." Use a hand-held mirror to take a regular look at your pussy. See if you can share images with your friends, especially if you are black. The internet has plenty of non-pornographic images of female genitalia, (best to search for yoni rather than vagina or pussy to avoid the porn) in all their various shapes and sizes, however most of the images are Caucasian and Asian.

128. While you are getting used to the look of a yoni, immerse yourself in other objects that mimic its form. Many flowers actually look like female genitalia, and why shouldn't they since flowers are the genitalia of plants. Buy flowers, such as orchids, for your home or office; get yourself some seashells, you'd be amazed how often shells look like women's genitals; have some oysters; start spotting how many things in the natural world mimic female genitalia. I have spotted flowers, tree trunks, crevices in boulders; in fact, if you can, take a picture and email it to me.

Get acquainted with your sexual energy.

129. If you don't, start masturbating. If you do, start doing it consciously. Often women approach masturbation in a very masculine manner. We tend to make it about the destination, not the journey, focusing on achieving orgasm as quickly and efficiently as possible. Nothing wrong there, it releases tension and relaxes the body. However, I would also like you to approach it as a love-making session with yourself, not like an inexperienced, grabby boy. Seduce yourself. Make time when you won't be disturbed. Set the scene. Maybe take a nice bath first and start the sensual experience there. Attend to all your senses. Have some sensuous food to tantalise your taste buds, light incense or put some fragrant

essential oils in your bath water, put on music, light candles. Go all out to set a seductive scene for yourself. When you do start touching yourself, start with your non-erogenous zones; your face, limbs, hands, feet, before you get to your neck, breasts and thighs, and finally your genitals. Even then linger on the outside for a while before you part your vulva and delve into the clitoris and vagina. All the while be aware of your sexual energy, remain in your body. Allow yourself to experiment with your breath – deep and shallow breaths, slow and quick breaths – to see how they affect your arousal. Do the same with sounds. Throughout the experience pause to look at your yoni in the mirror to notice how it looks at various stages of arousal. It does change. Experiment with bringing yourself to orgasms through various routes, clitoral, vaginal, by stimulating your G-spot, etc. Feel free to use sex toys and as much lubrication as you need. As you learn more about your sexual energy and responses you can teach your lovers how to please you better. No more chocolate over sex.

You can call on the goddesses listed below during your self-pleasuring sessions. Notice how your sexual energy behaves depending on which goddess you have chosen to embody.

Name your pussy.

130. I would like you to approach your pussy like you would a conscious being. Do not automatically hurry to name it, first see if it will give you its name. In your meditation, connect with your genitals. Have a conversation with your pussy. Basically, get to know it first, before you name it. Do all the steps above before you name it.

131. If you are struggling to give a voice to your pussy, get acquainted with Eve Ensler's *The Vagina Monologues*[1] – through the play or through the book. You can host your own vagina monologues with your female friends.

Unblock your sexual energy

132. Heal your Sacral Chakra. The sacral (Svadhisthana) chakra is in the pelvic area and relates to the colour orange. Like all the chakras, you can heal it in various ways, for example through sound (toning and mantras), crystals, meditations and visualisations, exercises or yoga. For healing the sacral chakra, water is good as this chakra is governed by the element of water. The water element also governs dancing and belly dancing is an especially good form of dance to move blocked sexual energy.

133. Adorn your yoni. We always wrap the things that we value in great packaging. Pick a Friday, preferably one with a full moon, and make a bonfire with all your holey underwear and stretched out granny panties. Then treat yourself to a shopping spree exclusively for underwear that makes you feel like a sex goddess. Buy or make one very special piece that will be your equivalent of Aphrodite's magic girdle. Aphrodite's husband, Hephaestus, made her an exquisite magical girdle of finely wrought gold, which, when she wore it, made Aphrodite irresistible to gods and men alike. What was he thinking? You can awaken your own feminine sexuality and link to the divine feminine by wearing a girdle dedicated to Aphrodite.

134. Divine Inspiration: When it comes to sexuality and sensuality there is a whole legion of goddesses you can enlist to help you own your sexy. My favourites are Aphrodite, Freyja, Ishtar and Oshun.

"Cheshire Puss," she began, rather timidly, as she did not at all know whether it would like the name: however, it only grinned a little wider. "Come, it's pleased so far," thought Alice, and she went on. "Would you tell me, please, which way I ought to go from here?"

"That depends a good deal on where you want to get to," said the Cat.

"I don't much care where –" said Alice.

"Then it doesn't matter which way you go," said the Cat.

"– so long as I get somewhere," Alice added as an explanation.

"Oh, you're sure to do that," said the Cat, "if you only walk long enough."

Excerpt from *Alice's Adventures In Wonderland*
by Lewis Carroll

Live on Purpose

> When I stand before God at the end of my life, I
> would hope that I would not have a single bit of
> talent left, and could say, "I used everything you
> gave me."
>
> ~ Erma Bombeck

What is the point of you, Lily?

We are nearing the end of our adventure, Lily. If you take only
a couple of things out of bootcamp, make it these two: (1)
Invest in your relationship with yourself, love yourself fully and
unconditionally. Become your own cheerleader and best friend.
(2) Live on purpose. You will experience fulfilment in your life
to the extent that your life is in alignment with your life purpose.
Consider this word "purpose".

What is purpose?

The dictionary defines purpose as the reason for which anything
is done, created or exists. Synonyms for purpose include: reason,

point, goal, design, aim, function, object, intention, objective, motive. In her book *The Spirit of Intimacy*,[35] Sobonfu Some relates a tradition of the Dagara tribe of West Africa. When a Dagara woman reaches a certain stage of her pregnancy she goes through a ritual called a Hearing Ritual. The medicine (wo)man puts the expectant mother into a trance, then village elders speak to the unborn child of its purpose. They ask the child, "Why are you here?" Speaking through the mother, the child shares his or her purpose with the elders, who record it. From the moment the child is born, the village supports her purpose. She is surrounded with the things and people who will equip her with the necessary knowledge, experience and skills to accomplish that purpose. Often, the Dagara name their children to reflect their life purpose. A Dagara child grows up clear about the reason for her existence, the point of her life. There is intention in her actions; her choices are driven by a clear motive. She understands what objective she is here to achieve. She lives on purpose.

Ours is not a society that prioritises such things. If it were, describing one's life with words such as loving, passionate, blissful and fulfilling would be far more prevalent than the usual "it's okay", "I am fine", and "it could be worse." There is a saying, "The mass of men lead lives of quiet desperation and go to the grave with their song still in them." Lily, are you belting out your song or are you leading a life of quiet desperation?

Do you believe that you have a soul, Lily? If you do, you would be wrong. Your soul has you. Your spirit existed before you were born and will live on after your body expires. Surely, then, it is your spirit that has you and not the other way round. Now ask yourself this, "Why is my spirit having this human experience?" There must be a reason, a purpose for having this life; in this body, borne of these parents, under those conditions, with this history, this unique combination of talents, weaknesses, skills, passions and interests. If you look at it like this, it is hard to think that any of it is random, that you happened by chance or even worse, mistake.

Most of us find our purpose the long way around. With society's move away from communal living, we have lost out on most of our education regarding the meaning of life and how to do life. Very few of us have gone through any rites of passage. No one has taught us what being human is about; not even what being a woman is about. When we experience our menarche – first menstrual flow – we are not schooled on our creative and generative abilities. Instead, we are given instructions on how to use sanitary pads and are warned about unwanted pregnancies. With the exception of a few cultures, this education on womanhood is not even a process but an event, a once-off conversation. One single talk, about the least important bits, at that. Ceremony and ritual have been lost to us. Rituals are tools for attributing meaning to the passages between life stages. They help you approach transitions with clarity, respect, confidence and awareness. Rites of passage help you locate yourself within your own personal path and the collective path of your people. In communities of yesteryear we had people to learn from, who taught us and provided a model we could emulate. There were members of the community who were tasked with helping the youth to contextualise developmental stages – their reasons, implications, blessings and burdens.

Who taught you about sex, Lily? When you had sex for the very first time, how much did you know about it? How much did your partner know about it? Did you learn from a friend, who learned from a friend who stumbled across his uncle's porn stash? In the land of the blind, the one-eyed man is king. For all you know we could be doing it all wrong. Actually, the high numbers of inorgasmic women implies that perhaps we really have no clue what we are doing. Even if we have the glossy magazines to look to for technique, were you ever taught how to use sex to consciously manifest your desires? Do you ever have sex as spiritual communion, would you know how to? We are clueless on so many aspects of life. You could actually say that life is a lost art. Conscious living certainly is.

In the face of escalating violence against women, high HIV infection rates and absent fathers, many men grapple with what it means to be a man, and they don't know where to turn for answers. No one taught their fathers and uncles, nor their grandfathers before them. For many generations now, they've had to feel their way through manhood, with displeasing results. The same applies to us. What does it mean to be a woman? When do you become a woman? On the day of you first period? Is it really reasonable to consider a 12-year-old a woman just because she can fall pregnant, or is transition into womanhood a process, a guided process? Many of us find our answers in the media, whose primary purpose is to sell products and services. We are barely even taught how to birth or rear children. Whereas long ago, there were a multitude of things that a growing person was guided through, now it has all trickled down to only one thing: schooling, which cannot replace all that other life education. The school system was never designed to create wholesome, balanced, happy and fulfilled human beings; it's purpose is to churn out employable, productive workers. We go to school to be taught how to become employees and, to a large extent, stay employees. The rest of our education has fallen by the wayside. Where we had elders, rites, initiations, circles, guides and mentors, we now have celebrity role models and Google. Our society churns out people wired to lead lives of quiet desperation. I dare say, it is invested in us feeling empty, unfulfilled, directionless and disoriented. There are entire industries that are invested in us remaining victims of that constant, nagging, empty feeling. You know the feeling I am talking about. That longing and suspicion that something important is missing from your life; the one thing that will make everything else fall into place. It is a widespread human condition, which has spawned entire commercial industries. We attempt to appease it with money, status, power, possessions, experiences, relationships, children, sex, drugs, alcohol, gossip, gambling – the list is inexhaustible. Unfortunately none of these things work in the long term. Because this is not a longing for things, it won't be fulfilled by something you find outside of yourself and put into your life, it can only be quenched by something you find within yourself and put out to life. It is a longing for purpose.

In *The Seven Spiritual Laws of Success*,[36] Deepak Chopra shares that when his children were growing up he assured them that he did not care about their performance at school. He made it clear that their only responsibility was to pay attention to their passions, invest their energy into becoming good at the things they were passionate about, and to figure out how to use those skills to serve life. It echoes Buddha's teaching that "your work is to discover your work, and then with all your heart, to give yourself to it". That is so radically different from how most of us have gone about life. Look what happens at schools. If a learner gets straight A's in languages but sucks at maths, we enrol her for extra maths classes and supervise her maths homework. We don't give her good literature to cultivate her love for languages. We don't direct her to movies with great dialogue to feed her passion and show her what she can do with it. We don't send her to a foreign country to learn another language. We get her a maths tutor instead. We focus on her weaknesses at the expense of her strengths. After investing much effort, her F for maths turns into a C and the A's for languages drop down to a C because all her energy had to go into improving her mathematical abilities – and we all know that it is much harder to do things that you don't like. At the end of her school life, we are presented with a C student. An average human being who can join the legion of other average human beings who've had their talents and passions educated out of them.

To identify and pursue your purpose generally requires a lot of determination and willingness to swim against the tide. Everything about how our society currently works goes against it. For instance, your passions, which are key to your purpose, are located lowest on your list of priorities. Passion and pleasure are nice-to-haves, generally relegated to weekends, holidays and retirement. Responsible adults invest their prime time and years into hard work, mostly building someone else's dream. The pursuit of passion and pleasure is reserved for trust fund babies and people who've had the fortune to marry well, when in fact they are inextricably linked to your purpose. This is wonderfully demonstrated in the movie *Julie and Julia*, which we spoke about in Session 13.

Despite all these built-in obstacles, it is important that you live on purpose. It is why you are here. You have a mission to fulfil. We all do. Everybody is here to contribute something valuable and unique. That nagging emptiness has a job: to remind you to get on with the business of fulfilling your purpose. Once you live on purpose the emptiness abates, saving you a lot of angst, time and money. As Robert Byrne put it, "The purpose of life is a life of purpose." Living on purpose is the key to peace and fulfilment. It makes your life make sense. Your history, longings, strengths, and weaknesses, are contextualised. Your purpose makes you matter. Yet many people are afraid to pursue their purpose. As a coach, I have many people who come to me claiming that they have no clue what the purpose of their lives is and, if only they knew what it was, their lives would be much better. When I inform them that I can help them identify their purpose, eight out of 10 do a disappearing act. I don't think it is because of any fault on my part. Chuck Spezzano[37] leads me to believe that it is a common issue, "When I had been conducting therapy for about 10 years, I began to see something I had not noticed before. The problems my clients seemed to be dealing with were, for the most part, distractions, delays and deceptions. I became curious about what these problems were hiding and soon it was clear that most people's problems were a way of avoiding their purpose in life. This avoidance both trivialised their lives and took away their sense of direction. I began to see that about 85 per cent of all of our problems are part of this conspiracy against ourselves – a conspiracy against our purpose and greatness. When we find our sense of purpose, most of our problems seem to naturally fall away. Whatever problems remain are necessary to bring about the learning experiences related to and necessary for our purpose."

It really comes down to a fear of leaving our comfort zone, no matter how wanting it may be. These people run because they are afraid that their purpose may be too disruptive to the life they have already invested in. They are afraid of change, rejection and failure.

I've grown fond of you, Lily, so I'd really hate to see you run.

The land of WOWness

Your comfort zone

Let's clear up some of the common misconceptions and objections against the pursuit of one's purpose:

No. 1: I am probably going to hate it.

Your purpose is always something that gives you pleasure. What better way for your soul to get you to stick with it? Even when something is crucial and of obvious value, if you don't enjoy it you are unlikely to stick with it. Exercise is a great example. The doctor can prescribe exercise to lower your dangerously high blood pressure and avoid a stroke, but if you hate gym and you choose that as your form of exercise, despite the very compelling advantages of the exercise, you are likely to drop out. If you love the outdoors and you decide to take up beach volleyball or hiking, something that you enjoy, you are far more likely to integrate the exercise into your life happily and stick with it. It's the same thing with your purpose. The intention is that you see it through, so it is always something you enjoy and find fulfilling.

No. 2: There is only one right way to fulfil my purpose.

You can choose various ways to articulate any one Life Purpose. For instance, many people may have the mission to bring more beauty to the world and choose to fulfil it in various, very different ways – as an artist painting beautiful pictures to adorn walls, a hairdresser, an interior decorator, a landscape gardener, a cosmetic surgeon or a housewife who does flower arrangements as a hobby.

No. 3: I am going to have to make sacrifices.

Your purpose always involves service, and many people associate service with sacrifice. We conjure images of Mother Teresa working her skinny arse off, getting by on bare necessities, with nary a pair of Manolos to show for it, or stereotypical UN volunteers, with body odour issues, who can't afford rent. Sacrifice is not mandatory for service. In fact, service can be extremely rewarding. One of the laws covered in *The Seven Spiritual Laws of Success*, is the Law of Dharma. Dharma is Sanskrit for "Purpose in Life". This spiritual law states that each and every soul incarnates for a purpose unique to that soul, and it is when the soul fulfils its purpose that it experiences inner peace, joy and fulfilment. The Law of Dharma further teaches that we have taken manifestation in physical form to fulfil a purpose. You have a unique talent and a unique way of expressing it. There is something that you can do better than anyone else in the whole world, and for every unique talent and unique expression of that talent there are also unique needs. Using your unique talents in service of others honours your spirit. Albert Schweitzer, the Nobel Peace Prize winner, counselled, "I don't know what your destiny will be, but one thing I do know: the only ones among you who will be really happy are those who have sought and found how to serve."

There are three components to the Law of Dharma. The first says that each of us is here to discover our true Self. The second component is to express our unique talents. The third is service to humanity. When you combine the ability to express your unique talent with service to humanity, then you make full use of the Law of Dharma.

Serving is not only about working for the UN or running a soup kitchen. You can serve through the gift of laughter like comedians do, or entertainment, like actors; through music, teaching or beautifying the world. Anything that lifts the vibration of a living thing is serving that thing positively.

No. 4: I don't have what it takes.

The nice thing about dharma is that, because yours is unique to you, you were designed for it. It always involves your talents, passions and interests; the skills derived from challenges overcome; traits that come naturally to you; things that make your heart expand; activities you lose yourself in; things that you would happily do for free. Your fear-based ego will tend to convince you that your purpose is more than you can accomplish, but keep in mind that we don't so much do our purpose as it is done through us. You just need to get out of your own way. As Maya Angelou says, "A bird does not sing because it has an answer, it sings because it has a song." Your purpose is your song. You don't need to learn it, figure it out, or have guaranteed standing ovations. You just need to let it come through you.

No. 5: I won't be able to make a living from it.

Perhaps you can, perhaps you can't, but no one said you had to leave your job for it. If you can figure out a way to make a living out of it, that's a bonus!

No. 6: I wouldn't know where to start.

It is oh, so easy. Look at what you love doing or being, and simply figure out a way to use that in service. I remember some years back a biker named Seipei Mashugane rode through all nine of our provinces in nine days on her motorbike in order to raise awareness and funds for POWA – People Opposing Women Abuse. She did something she loved – riding – to serve people she cared about – abused women.

Fulfilling your purpose is the quintessential win-win scenario; you get to help others – people, animals, nature – while marinating yourself in a giant, juicy vat of WOWness. Pursuing your purpose has awesome benefits:

• Fulfilling your purpose allows you to have your own personal, meaningful definition of success. You no longer need to look to an external benchmark to determine if you are doing well or you are on the right track.

- Living your purpose unlocks feelings of peace, joy and fulfilment within you.
- Once you start pursuing your life purpose, that frustrating inner longing ceases because you are finally fulfilling your purpose for being here.
- A greater sense of ease, flow and effortlessness in your life. When you pursue your life purpose, it is like rowing downstream because you are doing what you are meant to be doing. You are in flow.
- Your purpose always involves your natural strengths, talents and interests, so you get an opportunity to play to your strengths and do what you love.
- You become more focused as a result of increased clarity.
- Identifying your purpose will reduce stress and confusion in your decision-making because you will have clarity in your direction.
- You become more effective because you have access to a lot more energy, which previously went into futile attempts to appease the inner longing.
- Fulfilling your life purpose allows you to make a positive contribution to life, and leave a legacy.
- Identifying your life purpose gives you the answer to the questions: "Why am I here?" and "What is the purpose of my life?"
- Napoleon Hill, author of *Think and Grow Rich*, interviewed 500 self-made millionaires when researching his book and he says that the common denominator among all those people was a definite, defined and written purpose.

Are you living on purpose, Lily?

Becoming a Goddess. Living on Purpose

135. Discerning your life purpose: Take some time when you won't be disturbed and, in your journal, answer the following questions:

    a. What would I do with my time if I did not have to work for a living?

    b. What would I do if I knew I couldn't fail?

    c. If I were to write my own eulogy at the end of my life, how would I like it to read?

    d. What do I enjoy doing? What activities do I find so engaging that I lose time when absorbed in them? I look up and hours have flown by.

    e. What causes am I passionate about?

    f. What are my talents and abilities – those things that come easily to me?

    g. If I lived to be 90 years old and they threw a party in my honour, what would I be recognised for, who would I have touched, who'd attend the party, who would host it and why?

    h. What kind of challenges have I transcended in my life? Often our biggest challenges are partly there to equip us with the required life experience to guide others through similar quagmires.

136. Decide on the what. Your purpose is like a GPS. It helps you get to where you want to go. No more getting lost or ending up in dead-end streets. As with any GPS you must enter a destination, know where you want to go. All the questions above will help you get a good sense of your purpose, but you still need to decide how you will go about fulfilling it. If, for instance, you feel that your life purpose is about saving the planet, it's a big planet and many things are going wrong with it. What do you want to start with? How will you go about it? Will you teach people about preservation, write a book, make a movie, organise demonstrations, or work at

a reserve? You must decide how you choose to pursue your purpose.

137. Divine Intervention: Ask Hawaiian goddess of volcanoes, Pele, to ignite your passions and motivation to fulfil them in service of others, and Artemis to inspire you with a willingness to walk your own path.

"Come to the edge," she said.
They said, "We are afraid."
"Come to the edge," she said.
They came.
She pushed them... and they flew.

~ Guillaume Apollinaire ("he" remixed to "she" by me)

Just Do It

Don't be afraid your life will end; be afraid that it will never begin.

~ Grace Hansen

Lily, are you ready to trade OKness in for WOWness?

As I write this, I have recently left a stable, well-paying job because it prevented me from fulfilling my purpose. For years, I happily used to run The Goddess Academy, write and speak, while working in the corporate world. Late last year my boss informed me that "high-level" executives are no longer allowed to pursue any other paying interest outside of their work at the company. It meant that I had to suspend my coaching, workshops and writing. I pleaded, negotiated, reasoned, begged and threatened to no avail. Eventually, I accepted that they were not going to budge. I enjoy marketing and I like media, the industry has great perks, such as free music concert tickets, but my job was just that: a job. One that was now making me miserable, whereas in the past it allowed me to earn a decent living while I got to do what really mattered to me – my Goddess Academy work. It changed from facilitating to impeding my purpose, since I was forced to give up the one for the other. Lily, I am not a trust fund baby, nor am I comfortably married to someone who can pay my bills while I skip about through fields of sunflowers. I need to earn a living. Despite that, being unable to do the things that I loved made me miserable. I started to resent my job. A big source of my WOWness had been cut off. Happy colleagues irritated me. I zoned out in meetings and played on my phone. I'd drive behind slow trucks on my way to work, not bothering to overtake them, and waste hours at the mall just roaming around trying on shoes – and I am not a fan of malls. In short, I was miserable. I decided to leave my job. I spread the word that I was looking to move and soon offers of jobs were coming through, but none of them appealed to me. I realised that I had become miserable when I could no longer write and coach, but in fact corporate life had stopped being fun years before. All the rewards of a corporate life; the status, power, fancy office, and hoards of sycophant subordinates have never appealed to me. So I asked myself, why am I doing this? The answer was, "Because you always have". That sounded like a sad reason to use up 40 hours a week of my life. I concluded that surely there must be another, less expensive, way to earn a living. So, Lily, not only did I leave my job, I decided to leave formal employment.

Was it scary? You bet! It still is, but fear is such an unfortunate reason not to do something. Many of our fears are merely a pessimistic response to the question "What if?" They are a reaction to a negative projection about the future, a future that may never come to pass, one of countless possible futures. We seldom encounter something to be really afraid of, like being hijacked at gunpoint or being cornered by a Parktown Prawn (if you are like the women in my family). Often it is a fear of something that may or may not happen at some point in the future. There is a saying that fear is an acronym for False Evidence Appearing Real. The problem with fear is that it keeps us small and pedestrian. Fear is often the reason we never get to do anything extraordinary. The sad thing is that most of our fears never materialise, for two reasons. Firstly, we usually let the fear stop us from acting in the first place, and secondly, the feared possibility is only one of numerous ways in which the future may unfold. The majority of our fears hardly ever have life-threatening consequences. At best you fail or have an unpleasant experience and you can dust yourself off and try again, or move on. I can discover that leaving formal employment for "funemployment" was a bad idea, and I will look for, and find, another job. Easy. The most important thing is that I will have taken a chance on myself and, as many elders will tell you, in life you often regret the things that you didn't do, not the things that you did do – because whether something works out in the way that you had hoped or not, there is always a valuable lesson to be had from the experience. At the very least you will discover something new about yourself, a worthwhile lesson.

Lily, you know what you want. You know your dreams, desires, passion and purpose. Is fear stopping you from taking action? Fear is defined as an unpleasant, often strong, emotion caused by anticipation or awareness of danger. When we anticipate fear, it often comes in these forms, which Donna McCallum[38] describes as the seven types of irrational fear:

1. Fear of the power of authority or not fulfilling the wishes of authority
2. Fear that you don't know enough
3. Fear of failure
4. Fear that you won't make money
5. Fear that you will lose the respect of a loved one
6. Fear of rejection by society
7. Fear of ill health or lack of physical wellbeing

As soon as you can identify what kind of fear is holding you back, you can address it. You can think of contingency plans to put in place or ways to address your fears, but ultimately the way to overcome a fear of something is to "just do it!"

Did you know that the brand Nike, with its famous "just do it" slogan is named after the Greek goddess of Victory? Few victories are achieved without action. Fear can paralyse you into doing nothing, while action can help you conquer your fears and empower you. You know that exhilarating and powerful rush you get from having conquered a fear. The nice thing is that once a fear has been conquered you can continue to draw on that strength to address other fears in your life. If I overcame that, I can surely overcome this. With every fear you conquer, your world becomes bigger. Businessman and philanthropist Sir John Templeton said, "Dreams, visions, ideas can play significant roles in our lives. They can entice, entertain, or inspire us to greatness. To bring them into reality, however, we must act! Cowardice and lack of faith can keep one from a chosen goal, but if the heart is strong and brave, you can add action to your dreams and make them real." He talks about courage, which is obviously a necessary trait in surmounting fear, but he also talks about faith.

My decision to leave employment was not easy. I was afraid that I wouldn't have enough money, I was afraid that I would fail, I was afraid that I would make a fool of myself and have to go back, cap in hand. But I was also miserable. I couldn't decide which of the two was a lesser evil. I knew deep down that I could not tolerate my circumstances for much longer, but I had no idea what I was getting myself into; it seemed that all I could do was take the leap and hope for the best. Except, hope felt like such a flimsy thing to pin my future on – which is probably why it's called a leap of faith, not a leap of hope. I then had an interesting encounter with a man in his sixties who related to me how he had been rich and he had been poor, and the only times that he had been happy, irrespective of his state of wealth, had been when he was doing things he was passionate about. It gave me goosebumps, because it was pretty random how I came to be chatting to that man, and this was the very issue I was grappling with. We went on to talk about other things. He is a playwright who was busy writing a movie script. He likened his movie to another called *Divine Intervention*, which I had never heard of. When we parted, he called out and asked me to watch *Divine Intervention*. Our encounter felt like such surreal, divine intervention that I decided to look for the movie. I Googled it, only to find that it is an obscure, African American B-grade flick, which did not bode well for my chances of getting hold of it. At this point my phone rang. It was a friend who happened to be at a mall. I told him about my meeting with the playwright and this movie that I felt compelled to watch. He walked into the video shop while we were still chatting on the phone, asked if they had *Divine Intervention*, and lo and behold, they did! The message the movie had for me was about hope and faith – that often, to reach for your dreams, you require hope and faith. At the time, I was very hopeful but I had not factored faith into my plans. So I started talking to God(dess), explaining that I needed to leave my job and I had no clue what would be on the other side of salaried employment, but I was putting my faith in Spirit to look out for me. Soon after this, I got a call asking me to write this book. So I had one sure thing to do after employment. I took that as a sign from Spirit to "go ahead, I got you". I have since become quite big on praying: I ask for support, help and guidance on all sorts of things, big and small. Before, I used to reserve my praying for what I considered the big things; now I even have quick prayers for good parking spots. It's the faith that allowed me to take the leap. I don't think it matters much what you place your faith in, just that you believe in something over and above yourself, because there are always moments when your belief in yourself wavers.

Lily, now that you can label your fears so that you can address them, and you have a prescription for hope and faith to help you face them, we are ready to realise your dreams, wishes and desires.

First you should write them out as intentions. Turning a dream into an intention invites the universe to assist in its co-creation. This is the Universal Law of Intention. In her book *A Little Light on the Spiritual Laws*,[39] Diana Cooper describes it as follows: "Intention releases a force that makes things happen... you should be like an archer in setting your intentions. An archer pulls his bow back and holds it 'in tension' as he aims at his target before unleashing the arrow. The Law of Intention promises that whatever your aim, if you sight your target and invest your energy, the power of the universe will be unleashed behind your vision." As you can see, there is a fundamental difference between a desire and an intention. An intention has a different quality to a desire. A desire is something you wish would happen, an intention is something that you plan to realise. Be clear on your intentions and write them down. I often write out my intentions in my journal, and then I make a vision board with nice images, and words representing the things I choose to manifest. Sometimes I even pick a theme and a goddess to represent my intention. At various times, I have elected different goddesses to preside over my goals, such as Nike to give me a can-do attitude, Aphrodite to help me get in touch with my femininity, Isolt to assist in healing my heart and currently, when I write, I invoke Saraswati, the Hindu goddess of the arts. Sometimes I even select a theme song. Years ago, when I decided to come out of a period of social hibernation, I rocked to Diana Ross's "I'm Coming Out". You get the drift, Lily? Make your intentions multi-layered and pervasive. When there are multiple layers to your goals they become infinitely more attainable. A goddess, visual collage and a song are far more compelling than a goal that is only written. Use you womanly talents to find creative ways to make your goals rich and colourful.

Lily, I am about to share with you a secret to dramatically improve the chances of attaining your goals. Look beyond what you want to why you want it. Your motivation is your true goal. Many people would love to become millionaires, for example. In fact few people would turn down a seven-figure bank balance, but for a range of reasons. Some will want the money so they can leave their job or marriage, meaning what they actually want is freedom. Others may want a million so they can stop worrying about their bills, retirement or children's education – they want to feel secure. Yet others may want to become millionaires because they reckon people will take them seriously if they had a lot of money – what they really want is to feel powerful or worthy. None of them really wants lots of money; they all want a particular emotional state – freedom, security, esteem, and so on.

If you examine the motivation behind your desire, it is always an emotional state. Becoming a millionaire may be one way to feel powerful, but probably not the most easily attainable way, and certainly not the only way. When you realise that what you actually want is a sense of empowerment (an emotional state) not money (a thing) you get an opportunity to explore various ways to attain that emotional state.

The second reason to focus on the motivation/emotion is that you can make use of the Law of Attraction to help you manifest your desire. The law states that energy attracts like energy. Your energy is determined by your thoughts, through your emotions. Say you desire lots of money because you covet the freedom it will bring you. If you find other ways to feel free, it will reflect in your energy, and your energy of freedom will attract other things that you associate with freedom – such as a lot of money. It's a cool paradox. As soon as you don't need the money or relationship or better job – because you found another way to create the feeling – you dramatically increase your chances of attracting it, with ease. As Gandhi said, "You cannot have what you want, you can only have what you are." That is precisely how the Law of Attraction works; it brings together and delivers to you things that are like you.

It is worth your while to really grasp how the Law of Attraction operates. Having said that, Lily, I really wish *The Secret* had remained a secret.

In the late 1600s, Isaac Newton observed an apple fall from a tree, and got to wonder about why things fell down, never up. This led him to study the phenomenon he named the Law of Universal Gravitation or Gravity. Newton didn't invent gravity; things had been falling down for ages. He noticed, studied, labelled and publicised the Law of Gravity, but he did not cause things to start falling down instead of rising up. The same applies to *The Secret* and the Law of Attraction (LOA). The LOA has been in existence for aeons, long before *The Secret* or even other LOA classics, such as *Ask and It Is Given*[40] by Esther and Jerry Hicks.

I encounter many people who, having seen or read *The Secret*, have erroneously concluded that all they need to do to manifest their dreams is excel at thinking about them. Just visualising the things they want (previously known as day dreaming or fantasising) was not enough before *The Secret*, so why would it be enough now? After all, the LOA existed before *The Secret*.

I subscribe fully to the LOA. I believe that your thoughts do create your reality. I also believe that a big part of the manifestation process is action. Your thoughts create your emotions.

Jane and Thembi were at Tasha's waiting to meet up with their friend, Zai. They both received a text message from Zai, who is often tardy, saying she was stuck in traffic and would be half an hour late. Jane then thought, "Zai always underestimates the traffic and ends up being late for everything. She just can't seem to adjust to the heavy, big city traffic". Thembi, on the other hand, thought, "Zai is always late. She seems to think her time is more valuable than ours. I am sick and tired of always waiting for her. I bet she is more than 30 minutes away." This train of thought led to Thembi feeling angry, irritable and indignant, while Jane felt mild amusement and sympathy for Zai.

The emotions you feel, in response to the thoughts you have, determine how you will act and thus the reality you experience. Jane and Thembi's emotions produced two very different (re)actions. Jane chose to use the half hour wait to catch up on her emails. Thembi decided to vent her anger by refusing to wait for Zai. She stormed off and ended up stuck in the very traffic that had delayed Zai, causing her even more irritation. These two started with the same incident, but ended up with two very different experiences, because they took different actions in response to different emotions, based on different thoughts about the same thing.

This is primarily how we create our reality with our thoughts: we do it through our actions. Actions are the bridge between the inner world of thoughts and emotions and the outer world of experienced reality. Passive daydreaming about your dreams will get you exactly where it got you before *The Secret*: nowhere.

You are going to have to act, Lily.

Becoming A Goddess: Turning Dreams into Actions

138. Identify the fear holding you back. Where you are stuck there is probably fear. Especially if you find yourself procrastinating, or doubting yourself. Do two things:

    a. Doubt your doubt. We tend to doubt everything but doubt. Practice doubting your doubt.

    b. Find out what you are afraid of. Ask yourself, "What is my fear here?" What is the worst that I wish to avoid? It is easier to come up with strategies to overcome your fear when you are clear about what it is.

139. Use your attention wisely. Ask yourself, "What is the best thing that can happen in this situation?" Use this vision to motivate you. Focus your attention on this picture, what you want, not what you fear. Refer to session 11.

140. Cultivate hope and faith.

141. Ask. We reside in a co-creative world. In this realm, all creation is co-created. There is absolutely nothing that you can create by yourself. For instance, to make a baby you require the co-operation of a man and Spirit. Heck, you can't even make a cup of coffee on your own! Dr Carl Sagan, a scientist, cleverly observed, "If you want to make an apple pie from scratch, you must first create the universe." Hence, it is impossible to realise your desire when you are not open to receiving help. Ask for help. Learn to receive it. Refer to session 12.

142. Upgrade your desires to intentions.

    a. Write them out on a piece of paper and put them somewhere you will be able to see them often. State them as an intention: In 2013 I intend to travel to India – or even better, as a past-tense statement, "I had an amazing trip to India in 2013". Do not underestimate the power of this exercise. As long as there is true intention, as opposed to mere desire, powering it, sometimes the universe decides to do most of the work. I once had an intention to be featured in a particular magazine. I included it in my list of top 10 intentions for that year and forgot about it. Halfway through the year I got a call from a publicist informing me that the magazine wanted to do a feature on me!

b. Create a vision board and place it somewhere you can see it regularly.

c. Dream journaling. Write about your desire in your journal as if it has already happened. For example, "I am so glad to be back home putting my feet up! Today was hectic. We have begun shooting the third season of my cooking show. It has been a phenomenal success..."

d. Do a raindance. A raindance is the oral equivalent of dream journaling. When you are raindancing you talk about your desire as if it has already happened. Refer to session 15.

143. Just do it.

144. Divine Intervention: I'm sure Nike, the Greek Goddess of victory, will be happy to help you take action to realise your dreams, desires and purpose.

Commit to You

Self-love is moody. Much like our love for the
significant others in our lives, its intensity ebbs and
flows. Writing a formal vow reminds us of the truth
about ourselves when we forget.

~ Patricia Lynn Reilly

Is there an SLA between you and you, Lily?

I've learned to live by SLAs – service level agreements. Since we
can only do so many things at one time, be in only one place at a
time, and master only so many trades, we outsource many services
to other people and organisations. For instance, most companies
and households are not keen on cleaning up after themselves, so
they hire cleaning companies or maids respectively. Similarly, most
businesses exist to sell their products and services, but very few
create their own advertisements. They usually hire communications
or advertising specialists to conceptualise and produce their print,
radio and TV ads. When you see in-house ads made by the boss's

nephew, who is artistic, you usually understand why sticking to your knitting is a good idea. Whether you like it or not, it is hard to conduct life without outsourcing many crucial roles. This, however, opens you up to the disappointment of poor delivery. This is where SLAs come in. They clearly articulate your respective responsibilities, and expectations of delivery and conduct. Be it your children's nanny or the IT company, if there is no SLA in place the relationship can deteriorate rapidly.

As a manager, whenever someone informed me that they were unhappy with a supplier's performance, I always asked them how they were managing the relationship with the supplier. Often dissatisfaction arises because no clear standards are in place. SLAs force you to think about the purpose of the relationship, what is expected of all parties and the acceptable level of delivery. When you think about it, this applies to all your relationships, not just outsourced, professional ones. Your friends, children, partners and relatives benefit greatly when they are clear on what is expected of them, along with what is acceptable and unacceptable to you. You probably don't make your beloved initial 20 pages of a legally drafted SLA – though sometimes you may wish you had – but you've probably established a tacit SLA of some sort. They know to call when they are running late, or that you expect them to deal with all car-related issues, or that they cannot disappear for the whole weekend when your family comes to visit, for instance. If a relationship is important to you personally and professionally, a clearly thought-out SLA is highly recommended.

The most important relationship you have is with yourself. This relationship influences all the other relationships that you have. Remember the Law of Correspondence: as within, so without. All other relationships, be they with other people, money, things, even with Spirit, are a reflection of your relationship with yourself. If you get this one relationship right, you get your world right. This is the longest relationship you will have. This is the only person in the entire world you spend every moment with. As discussed in session 16, this relationship creates your world and affects how you experience your life in it. Your relationship with yourself is everything. If ever a relationship required an SLA, this would be the one. If all is well in this relationship, automatically all becomes well in your world. If there is no clear SLA in place, you can easily find yourself in a position where you progressively, and insidiously, slide into giving yourself very bad service.

As part of my IAW Facilitator-Coach training,[41] I got an opportunity to examine my relationship with myself and to determine my expectations and standards for the relationship going forward. I then wrote vows to myself, for maximum love, care, honour and respect, which I took in a self-commitment ceremony.

I share my original vows with you with the aim of inspiring you to make, and keep, your own promises to yourself.

I, Kagiso Muntu Msimango, vow to open up to life. I built walls to protect me, instead they imprisoned me. Now I bring them down. This is my pledge; to say "YES!" to life.

I, Kagiso, pledge to be gentle with myself. To love, accept and forgive myself, over and over again, all the days of my life. Akin to the beautiful lotus flower which grows out of mud, I vow to seek the gems in "bad" experiences, and thus free myself of regrets.

The allure of perfection shall not intimidate me or hinder my growth, since I vow to love myself with the same intensity through hits and misses.

I vow to stop entertaining these two questions:
1.   "What is wrong with me?"
2.   "Who is going to save me?"
They lead me away from the truth. There is nothing wrong with me, there never was and never shall be, consequently I do not require a saviour. Henceforth, I promise to make choices that are reflective of this truth.

I vow to trust myself; to value my personal truth over the truth of others. I know better what is best for me. I pledge to appreciate my personal experience, valuing its lessons above the expectations and prescriptions of others.

I vow to give my feelings and intuition the same credence I give my intellect: To honour the inherent validity of ALL my feelings. I give myself permission to base my decisions solely on how I feel.

With courage, I vow to feel ALL my feelings, not to block, minimise or attempt to hang on to those that have dissipated.

This promise I make to myself: to act courageously in expressing my truth, to myself and others.

I vow to accept my needs, wants, dreams and desires without judgement, whether I choose to pursue their fulfilment or not.

I vow to remain loyal to myself all the days of my life; to never choose the love, acceptance or approval of another over my own. I promise to never abandon or demote my relationship with myself for any other role.

I vow to recognise as a liar any voice, internal or external, that tells me that I am inferior to or superior to another.

I vow to never ask another for that which I am not giving to myself. I take responsibility for meeting my own needs, even as I enlist the support and help of others and learn to achieve a balance between independence and interdependence.

I vow to heal my relationship with my body. To remember that my body is much more than a set of measurements; it is a vital conduit for my physical experience, a guardian and a teacher. I vow to love and nurture my body, to befriend, honour and respect it and to listen to its wisdom all the days of my life.

I intend to remember that I am a creative being, who imagines her reality into being, and behave accordingly, giving my powers of co-creation the respect that they deserve. I will nurture and regularly express my creative impulses.

I promise to embrace and celebrate my femininity. To be curious about its gifts. To explore feminine gentleness, creativity and intuition. To love my woman body, its softness, curves and receptivity.

All in all, I, Kagiso, pledge to value myself; respecting my body, needs and desires and honouring my body, mind, emotions and spirit.

This is it.[42]
This is my life.
Nothing to wait for,
Nowhere else to go,
No one to make it all different
This is it.
What a relief to have finally landed. Here... now.
Blessed be my life.

And so it is.

Becoming a Goddess: Committing to Yourself.

145. Honestly and critically examine your relationship with yourself.
    a. Think about all the things you consider in a happy, healthy relationship and place your relationship to yourself against those standards.

    b. Look at what is important to you and examine whether the way you are currently living is in alignment with what matters to you.

    c. Look at how people you admire treat themselves.

    d. Consider all the things you've learned about yourself during bootcamp in relation to what you aspire to.

146. Based on your findings, construct an SLA, made up of vows to yourself.

147. Commit to you: Create a commitment ceremony where you will take these vows. Have witnesses. You can be as elaborate or as simple as you like in the ceremony. Follow your intuition.

148. Ask for help: If you are struggling with any of these steps, The Goddess Academy facilitates this entire process.

149. Divine Intervention: Invite any of the goddesses that you resonate with to support you in composing and upholding your vows.

Be Okay with OKness

Gorgeous goddess, we have come to the end of goddess bootcamp. There is enough within these pages, including 149 actions, to empower, inspire and support you to create a fabulous purpose-led life of WOWness that is powered by passion and positively oozes with pleasure. The process of writing this book led me to re-member long-lost parts of myself, from both the light and the shadow, yet all unimaginably mine. For this unexpected gift that you have unwittingly bestowed upon me, I would like to reciprocate with some parting counsel.

Be okay with the very OKness that led you to conjure this book.

This may sound paradoxical considering the time and energy bootcamp has devoted to leading you out of the middling republic of OKness. Yes, access to the land of WOWness requires change. Change in your choices, beliefs, actions and expectations. Yet, to change your life from drab to fab, you will have to be okay with its current state of OKness. The goddess way to positive transformation is through making peace with what is. Before you go for more, better or different, be okay with things as they are now. Love, accept, appreciate and be grateful for every single aspect of your life exactly as it is right now. Honour it. Seek the magic in your difficult marriage, the lessons delivered by your failing health, how your boss's fuckwittery is serving you, and the gifts of all the imperfections in your life, so you can be okay with it all.

There is a feminine strategy that some clever women employ to keep their men from straying that I absolutely love. Many women who have attractive partners who are not particularly motivated to remain sexually faithful have become veterans in the wily ways of subtle "home defending". Having tried everything, the intelligent ones soon learn, and eventually accept, that you cannot control another person. Instead of wasting their energy threatening and patrolling wayward lovers, they have developed perceptive radar with which they detect their partners' potential future lovers. You know what they do when they spot one? They don't drive her out of town. They befriend her. This has a better success rate than making an enemy out of her, and it is not at all about keeping your friends close and your enemies closer. Like you, those potential future mistresses of your beloved can tell when someone is not being genuine. So the "home defender" truly finds things to like about this other woman. She seeks to build a real connection and true empathy. If they succeed in establishing a genuine connection, more often than not, the potential "other" woman becomes less inclined to play "hide the sausage" with their Casanova. I know a woman who is married to an impossibly attractive and charming Lothario. She has a whole harem of friends she acquired through her attempts to neutralise her husband's amorous charms. What really blows my mind is that she has genuine friendships with these women. Consider this approach to all aspects of your life you've marked for change.

Have you noticed what happens when you start yelling at

yourself for gaining weight? You feel hungry and just want to stuff yourself with ice cream and cupcakes. Same thing happens when you are catty to the woman whose panties your lover is attempting to drop, she will happily sleep with him because "shame, his woman" – that's you – "is such a bitch". When you berate yourself for not studying, instead of feeling energised to get through your assignment, you inexplicably start feeling sleepy. When you make an enemy out of your problem, it returns the favour and strikes back. To free yourself of any circumstance, first you must embrace it and acknowledge that is has value. Just as butterflies have to first pay their dues as icky caterpillars and the exquisite lotus flower grows out of mud, you too need some ickyness and what-the-fucks to metamorphose into the goddess you were always destined to become. You needed some discomfort and dissatisfaction with your current circumstances to motivate you to want something different for yourself.

Through all changes, be gentle with yourself. Do not berate yourself for the mistakes that got you here nor allow yourself to be embittered by the misfortunes that befell you. View yourself and your circumstance with a generous heart. I don't know the circumstances that led you to conjure this book, whether your life was simply bland from mediocrity or seriously bitter from more unfortunate events, but I do know that to get to your future you must befriend your present. To escape OKness for the yummy land of WOWness, you need to be okay with where you are right now, what you have, who you are with, what you are doing and who you are being. It makes the journey to WOWness feel like a fun road-trip of learning and self-discovery instead of a hellish journey of strife, shame and guilt.

The way of the goddess is one of pleasure. If it's not fun then you are not doing it right. In that case, call me.

Wishing you effortless joy.
Kagiso

Goddess Bootcamp Crew

Meet the ancient goddesses mentioned throughout goddess bootcamp.

Artemis: (Diana to the Romans)
Artemis is the Greek goddess of the hunt and the moon. She is an independent, free spirit, who chose to run free in the woods with her posse of hounds and wood nymphs, instead of getting married and settling down.

Athena: (Minerva to the Romans)
Beautiful warrior goddess, Athena was the only Olympian goddess portrayed wearing armour. She is the Greek goddess of wisdom and craft. She presided over battle strategy during times of war and over arts in times of peace.

Aphrodite: (Venus to the Romans)

Aphrodite the Greek goddess of love and beauty, was born fully formed, after her father's castrated genitals were cast into the sea. As such she represents unashamed sexual energy. She chose Hephaestus as her husband, however this did not stop her from indulging in passionate affairs with gods, such as Ares the god of war, and mortals, such as Adonis, alike. Aphrodite was completely comfortable with her body and sexuality and can help you do the same. She loved being nude, and it is clear from her numerous affairs that she also loved sex. She enjoyed lovers of both genders. If you have any sexual hang-ups you would like to shake off, then Aphrodite is your girl.

Bast: Egyptian goddess of play, pleasure, music, partying and cats. She was the ruler of the city of Bubastis, where it is said almost everyone owned a cat. As the goddess of fun times, a massive festival was held in her honour on 31 October. She is often depicted with a sexy female body and a cat's head, holding a sistrum, an ancient musical instrument.

Baubo: A wild Greek goddess associated with sacred sexuality and laughter. Baubo is credited with lifting Demeter's dark mood after she had fallen into a deep depression as a result of her daughter, Persephone's abduction by Hades, god of the underworld. Baubo lifted Demeter's depression by playing the fool and literally lifting her skirt. This goddess does not take herself and her sexuality too seriously.

Brigid: Brigid is a Celtic triple goddess, meaning she represents the three aspects of the divine feminine – maiden, mother and crone. She was such a popular goddess of the hearth, fertility, healing and creativity, that when Christianity "took over" she came along as St Brigit of Kildare, with a temple in Ireland. She is still celebrated on the Imbolc, 1 February, marking the beginning of spring in the Northern hemisphere.

Butterfly Maiden: To Native American tribes such as the Hopi, Zuni and Navajo, Butterfly Maiden is believed to bring about new beginnings and transformations. Like the butterfly, she represents metamorphosis. She is the goddess of fresh starts, a symbol of rebirth and regeneration.

Cerridwen: A Welsh moon goddess of magic, she once turned a clumsy assistant into a hen and proceeded to eat him. Nine months later she gave birth to him. As a result she is also associated with death and rebirth.

Durga: Durga is an ass-kicking Hindu goddess who was conjured by the gods to help them fight Mahishasura, the demon who threatened the world. She destroyed the demon and restored order to the cosmos.

Eostre: This Germanic goddess, from whom the names of East, Easter and oestrogen are derived, is a fertility goddess and goddess of the dawn, who would ride up on a rainbow each year and bring forth Spring.

Eve: Eve is our Biblical foremother, who chose not to stay in her little corner as she was instructed to do. If it wasn't for Eve we would still be stuck in that nasty garden having sex in the missionary position, with Lord knows what kind of creepy crawlies accessing our lady parts, including Adam.

Freyja: The Nordic goddess of love, war, fertility and celebration, Freyja's name means "The Lady". She was the leader of the Valkyries, and considered one of the most beautiful and powerful deities in the Norse pantheon. Friday is named after her – Freyja's day. She was completely comfortable with her sexuality, and was something of a Vixen. She was married to Od whom she loved deeply, but she had numerous lovers. Freyja travelled in style, in a chariot pulled by two beautiful and formidable cats given to her by Thor. She had an enchanted necklace known as the

Brisingamen, made of gold, rubies and amber. When she wore it, no one could resist her charms. Freyja can help you to create a symbolic Brisingamen of your own, to help you release your natural magnetism.

Gaia: (Terra to the Romans)
The Greeks worshipped Gaia as the embodiment of the earth. She embodies every living thing on earth, from tiny ants to imposing redwood trees. She is the primordial great mother, commonly known as Mother Earth.

Ishtar: (Inanna to the Sumerians)
Ishtar was an extremely sexual goddess who aligned her sexuality strongly with spirituality. In ancient times, people used to commune with the Divine through sex. There were priestesses whose vocation was to have sex with men, to facilitate communion with God through the union of the god (male) and goddess (female) aspects of the Divine. These sex priestesses lived in temples where sacred sex rituals took place and they were Ishtar's charges. The Middle East was populated with numerous Ishtar temples. Ishtar was very popular, clay figurines of her have been unearth throughout the Middle East. They depict Ishtar as voluptuous with big breasts, fleshy thighs and some serious junk in her trunk. Ishtar taught that anyone who denies sex denies life, because sex facilitates creation, and creation represents God.

Isolt: Isolt, the Celtic goddess of love, is the daughter of an Irish King and a druid Priestress. She was caught in a love triangle between her husband, King Mark of Cornwall, and the handsome knight, Sir Tristan. Because of her experiences, Isolt now helps in all matters of the heart, healing a broken heart and assisting with romantic, platonic and parental relationships.

Ixchel: Together with her husband the sun god, Itzamna, Ixchel the moon goddess, gave birth to all the other Mayan gods. She controls water and rain, and is also known as Lady Rainbow.

Kali: Kali is a super-powerful goddess. According to Hindu legend, she is the mother of us all. She is both the gentle mother and the fierce warrior. She is also known as a goddess of destruction, but she only destroys for purposes of renewal, and new, better beginnings.

Kuan Yin: Kuan Yin a bodhisattva, meaning she is eligible for Buddhahood. She has vowed to stay near the earth until all of earth's beings are enlightened. She is the goddess of Mercy and Compassion. Many consider her the Mother Mary of the East. You can connect with her by chanting *Om Mani Padme Hum*, (pronounced Ohm mah-nee pahd-may hoom).

Lilith: According to Hebrew legend the first woman God created, alongside Adam was the strong-willed Lilith. Both of them were created from the same materials, so Lilith considered herself Adam's equal. Adam, on the other hand, expected Lilith to always "lie beneath him" literally and figuratively. Lilith was having none of that, so she left Adam and was replaced with Eve.

Mother Mary: Mary is the virgin mother of Jesus Christ. She is the representation of the divine mother in the Christian west.

Nemetona: A very ancient goddess of the Celts. Nemetona was worshipped primarily in what is now France and Germany, but her worship extended into England, where there is an altar dedicated to her in Bath. Her name means "sacred space" because she protected the Celt's ceremonial sites. She watches over sacred sites, especially those connected with nature.

Ninavanhu-Ma: She is the Mother Goddess that the renowned Zulu traditional healer Credo Mutwa speaks of in his book *Indaba, My Children*. He tells a creation myth, where the silver-coloured Ninavanhu-Ma with golden eyes and four breasts each with an emerald nipple, created the human race.

235

Oshun: She is a Yoruban goddess who presides over love, sex, beauty, wealth and diplomacy. She protects the area around the sacral chakra. Amongst many other things, she teaches her devotees how to be comfortable with their sexuality, and to be playfully flirtatious. She is also goddess of the sweet (fresh) waters, whereas Yemaya rules the salt waters.

Oya: In Yoruban mythology Oya is the goddess of the Niger River, storms, tempests and rain. She is known to create chaos in order to unearth the underlying calm. In Yoruba the word Oya literally means "she tore". She fosters change through chaos and destruction. Oya is a goddess of transformation.

Pandora: Pandora is the very first woman in Greek mythology. Pandora's most famous tale is of Pandora's box, which is similar to that of Adam, Eve and the forbidden fruit. In Pandora's case she and her husband were given a gift box by her father Zeus and instructed not to open it. Curiosity got the better of Pandora and despite her husband's objections she opened the box and out flew all kind of disease, hate, envy, and all the bad things that people had never experienced before but are now plagued by.

Pele: Pele is an ancient Hawaiian goddess who lives in the world's most active volcano – Kīlauea Volcano. She is feared by those who misunderstand her, due to her fiery eruptions. Legend has it that her father sent her away from Tahiti because of her hot temper. Yet her fiery nature – she is passionate, volatile and capricious – can be harnessed to light up your own passion and energise you.

Saraswati: This daughter of Lord Shiva and Goddess Durga is the goddess of arts and knowledge. She has four hands representing four aspects of human personality in learning: mind, intellect, alertness and ego. Saraswati is happy to help with all creative expressions, such as music, writing, and dancing. Her birthday – *Vasant Panchami* – is a Hindu festival celebrated every year on the fifth day of the lunar month of *Magha*.

Spider Woman: To Native American cultures like the Navajo and Hopi, Spider Woman is the mother of all creation. She is the mother goddess who sits in the middle of the universe spinning her web, connecting all living things to each other.

Sulis: Celtic sun goddess who oversees bodies of water associated with healing. She is the Goddess of the hot springs at Bath, England (the only hot spring in Britain). Her hot spring has been renowned for its healing powers since ancient times, and when the Romans arrived in Britain they built a bath complex around the springs, and named the place Aquae Sulis – the Waters of Sulis.

Yemaya: The Yoruban mother of water, Yemaya's name is a contraction of *Yeye Omo Eja*, which means "mother whose children are the fish". As all life is believed to have come from the sea, Yemaya is considered to be the mother of all. She was exported from her native West Africa and is now also worshiped as an Afro-Caribbean and Brazilian goddess where she is referred to as Yemanja.

Endnotes

Session 1: Seek the Goddess

1 *A Goddess Is a Girl's Best Friend* by Laurie Sue Brockway. Published by The Berkeley Publishing Group, 2002.

2 *Goddess: A Celebration in Art and Literature* edited by Jalaja Bonheim. Published by Stewart, Tabori & Chang, 1997.

Session 2: Happen to Life

3 Judah Isvaran is a Conscious Leadership Spiritual Practitioner based in Los Angeles, California.

Session 3: Know Thyself

4 *The Seven Spiritual Laws of Success* by Deepak Chopra. Co-published by Amber-Allen Publishing and New World Library, 1994.

Session 4: Choose You

5 Reversed price tags parable. Read in IAW Empowerment

Programme – Fundamentals VI: Love Your Body, by Patricia Lynn Reilly.

6 IAW – Imagine A Woman – is a life-coaching protocol designed by a woman, Patricia Lynne Reilly, administered by women, for women.

7 *The Gifts of Imperfection* by Brené Brown, PhD. Published by Hazelden, 2010.

Session 5: Change Only You

8 *The Dark Side of the Light Chasers* by Debbie Ford. Published by The Berkeley Publishing Group, 1999.

Session 6: It's Not All You

9 *Reviving Ophelia: Saving the Selves of Adolescent Girls* by Mary Pipher, PhD. Published by Riverhead Trade, 2005.

10 According to the National Institute of Mental Health, major depression and dysthymia affect twice as many women as men. This two-to-one ratio exists regardless of racial and ethnic background or economic status. The same ratio has been reported in twelve countries all over the world.

11 Datamonitor is an independent business information and market analysis company.

12 Credit goes to Patricia Lynne Reilly for bringing this issue to my attention. It never occurred to me that so many of our issues may be inherited until before studying for my IAW facilitator/ Coach certification.

13 *Be Full of yourself! The Journey from Self-Criticism to Self-Celebration* by Patricia Lynne Reilly. Published by Open Window Creations, 1998.

Session 7: Free Your Heart

14 Eckhart Tolle is the author of *The Power of Now* and *A New Earth*. In 2011, the *Watkins Review* listed him as the most spiritually influential person in the world.

15 TEDx are independently organised TED events, created in the spirit of TED's mission, "ideas worth spreading".

16 Howard Martin is one of the founders of HeartMath and co-author of The HeartMath Solution. He has been part of the HeartMath consulting team since its inception in 1991.

17 The Institute of HeartMath is a leading authority on stress and the physiology of emotions.

Session 8: Feed Your Soul

18 Chuck Spezzano, PhD is a world-renowned seminar leader, author, visionary and founder of Psychology of Vision. He holds a doctorate in Psychology.

19 Abraham has described them as "a group consciousness from the non-physical dimension". They are channeled by Esther Hicks and their teachings can be found in several books authored by Jerry and Esther Hicks.

Session 11: Say "Yes!" to Life

20 *The Seven Spiritual Laws of Success* by Deepak Chopra. Published by Amber-Allen Publishing, 1994.

21 Margot Anand is an internationally acclaimed authority on Tantra, best-selling author, and teacher and founder of SkyDancing Tantra.

Session 12: Learn to Receive, Graciously

22 David Deida is the author of hundreds of essays, audiotapes, videotapes, articles, and books on spirituality and sexuality. He is a founding associate of Integral Institute and has taught and conducted research at the University of California Medical School in San Diego; University of California, Santa Cruz; San Jose State University; Lexington Institute, Boston; and *Ecole Polytechnique* in Paris, France.

Session 13: Say "Yes" to Pleasure

23 Stellar Relationships and other teachings by the Vedic Astrologer, Sam Geppi can be found at samgeppi.com.

24 Joseph Campbell was an American writer and lecturer of mythology and comparative religion. His philosophy is often

summarised by the phrase "Follow Your Bliss".

25 "Dynamic spread of happiness in a large social network: longitudinal analysis over 20 years in the Framingham Heart Study" by James Fowler and Nicholas Christakis. Published in the *British Medical Journal* on 4 December 2008.

26 Joe Vitale is an American best-selling self-help author and star of *The Secret* movie.

Session 14: Travel Light

27 Chuck Spezzano, PhD is a world-renowned seminar leader, author, visionary and founder of Psychology of Vision. He holds a doctorate in Psychology.

28 Anaïs Nin was a French author who is famous for publishing erotic literature and her journals, *The Diary of Anaïs Nin*, which she began keeping at the age of 11.

Session 15: Mind Your Language

29 *The Four Agreements: A Practical Guide to Personal Freedom*, by Don Miguel Ruiz. Published by Amber-Allen Publishing, 1997.

Session 19: Love You, More

30 *The Gifts of Imperfection: Your Guide to a Wholehearted Life* by Brené Brown. Published by Hazelden, 2010.

Session 17: Embrace Your Femininity

31 Carl Jung was a Swiss psychologist and psychiatrist who founded analytical psychology. He contributed many ideas, which continue to inform contemporary life, such as complex, archetype, persona, shadow, anima and animus, personality typology, dream interpretation, and individuation.

32 *You Can Heal Your Life* by Louise L Hay. Published by Hay House, 1999.

Session 19: Own Your Sexy

33 From Devi Ward's website: Authentic Tantra www.deviward.

wordpress.com. *The Vagina Monologues* started as a play written by Eve Ensler, which ran in 1996. The play has since been staged internationally and even as a television series.

34 *American Journal of Obstetrics and Gynecology* Volume 175, Issue 3 (September 1996).

Session 20: Live on Purpose

35 *The Spirit of Intimacy: Ancient African Teachings in the Ways of Relationships* by Sobonfu Somé. Published by William Morrow Paperback, 2000.

36 *The Seven Spiritual Laws of Success* by Deepak Chopra. Published by Amber-Allen Publishing, 1994.

37 Chuck Spezzano, PhD is a world-renowned seminar leader, author, visionary and founder of Psychology of Vision. He holds a doctorate in Psychology.

Session 21: Just Do It

38 Donna McCallum is also known as the Fairy Godmother. She has helped thousands of people in South Africa, the UK and the US focus on their dreams and goals. She is the author of *The Fairy Godmother's Guide to Getting What you Want*.

39 *A Little Light on Spiritual Laws* by Diana Cooper.

40 *Ask and It Is Given* by Esther and Jerry Hick.

Session 22: Commit to You

41 To deepen your relationship with yourself, the IAW Empowerment Program invites you to compose a vow of faithfulness to your own life. A vow of faithfulness is a positive declaration, affirmation, or promise, expressing your intention to remain loyal to yourself, to preserve allegiance to yourself even when challenged and opposed.

42 This part is the closing blessing from IAW's self-commitment ceremony.

Born with an enquiring mind, Kagiso Msimango's constant questioning of the status quo landed her in therapy in her early 20s. Her psychiatrist advised her to accept that life is hard and prescribed antidepressants – the pharmaceutical equivalent of putting on your big-girl panties. Unwilling to accept life as something she needed to be medicated against, she turned her probing mind towards learning how not only to survive, but to thrive joyfully.

Studying psychology, metaphysics and energy healing, to help heal her own life, Kagiso then became a certified life coach and founded The Goddess Academy in 2006 to help other women inject a big dose of WOWness into their lives.